Special Little Knits from
JUST ONE SKEIN

CHERYL POTTER

Martingale®
& COMPANY

DEDICATION

In gratitude to my dear friend JoAnne Turcotte of Plymouth Yarn Company. JoAnne, this one's for you!

ACKNOWLEDGMENTS

I have to admit that writing and designing projects for this book was a lot of fun. Special kudos to the designers, who tried to squeeze every last row out of the yarns they were given and did not complain about ripping out and starting over. Thanks to all at Cherry Tree Hill, from hand dyers to yarn winders, pattern proofers, and those who tagged and bagged yarns and garments. And of course, thanks to the well-organized and creative group at Martingale & Company.

Special Little Knits from Just One Skein
© 2007 by Cheryl Potter

& C O M P A N Y

Martingale & Company
20205 144th Ave. NE
Woodinville, WA 98072-8478 USA
www.martingale-pub.com

Credits

CEO ~ Tom Wierzbicki
Publisher ~ Jane Hamada
Editorial Director ~ Mary V. Green
Managing Editor ~ Tina Cook
Developmental Editor ~ Karen Costello Soltys
Technical Editor ~ Carol A. Thelen
Copy Editor ~ Durby Peterson
Design Director ~ Stan Green
Illustrator ~ Robin Strobel
Cover and Text Designer ~ Stan Green
Photographer ~ Brent Kane

MISSION STATEMENT

Dedicated to providing quality products and service to inspire creativity.

Printed in China
12 11 10 09 08 07   8 7 6 5 4 3 2 1

Library of Congress Cataloging-in-Publication Data
Library of Congress Control Number: 2006035734

ISBN: 978-1-56477-719-5

CONTENTS

INTRODUCTION

HOW OFTEN HAVE YOU PURCHASED an odd skein of yarn because it looked lonely in a sale bin or because the colors and textures called to you, but you had no idea what to knit with it? How many single skeins of gorgeous yarn adorn your stash, never to be transformed into apparel because they match nothing and seem to have too little yardage to complete anything substantial?

As a knitter, I have had these experiences too many times to mention. Yet I continue to collect odd skeins for their texture and color, like exotic fruit. Sometimes I arrange them by fiber, sometimes by color, and often by baskets in a spare room.

Single skeins result from broken dye lots, and knitters refer to these skeins as "orphans." Although there is nothing wrong with the yarn itself, the skeins usually get sold as seconds. Any yarn can lose its family and become an orphan: solid yarns, machine-printed yarns, and hand-painted yarns alike.

Long ago, before I discovered that hand-painted yarn could be created in dye lots much like machine-processed yarn, I named my single skeins "one-hank wonders." I did not think of these hanks as orphans but as unique only children alone in the world by choice. Because I purposefully created single skeins, my goal was to ensure that a knitter could make an entire project from just one skein of yarn. Each skein was individually painted so that no two garments would look alike, lending each project unique appeal. My approach took years of refinement, because the downside was that the knitting remained unfinished if for some reason the garment could not be completed with the yarn at hand.

With proper pattern support and a working knowledge of yardage and gauge, any knitter can transform an orphan into a one-hank wonder. As long as you achieve gauge and your yarn has the same yardage, same weight, and similar fiber content as the single skeins used in this book, you can confidently create any of these garments without ripping out the knitting or adjusting to a smaller size.

Today, even hand-dyed yarn companies assign dye-lot numbers to painted yarns, although some resist this trend, preferring unique and individually processed skeins. Whether you desire to reduce or enhance your stash or to knit with solid or variegated yarns, please use the projects in this book as a resource guide and for inspiration. Don't hesitate about buying that one expensive skein of silk or the odd lot of ribbon. Your purchase can either age happily in your stash or, with the help of this book, be knit into a complete project right away.

We often think of a skein of yarn as a bundle coiled so that the yarn is pulled from the middle as we work, and we think of a hank of yarn as a loosely coiled loop. In this book, the terms skein and hank are used interchangeably.

Single skeins of yarn in various weights

Working with ONE SKEIN

THE IDEA FOR THIS BOOK came to me one sleepless night after a national yarn show. I could only marvel at how my tiny world of hand-dyed yarn had evolved into big business in my 10 years of showing Cherry Tree Hill yarn. When I first began painting yarn, for example, there was no such thing as a hand-painted dye lot. Knitters were expected to buy all their skeins of yarn at once from the same dye batch, if possible, or to try switching off similar-looking balls every two rows to spread various colors evenly. Few dared to let the yarn do its own thing and create variegated garments with pooled or concentrated colors. Today's knitters have no fear.

As a colorist, I spent years mastering the art of hand dyeing multiple skeins in a similar manner and thus creating a dye lot. In the meantime, I celebrated the uniqueness of each skein by creating patterns that were skein-specific, giving knitters an opportunity to finish an entire pair of socks from one skein of yarn, for example. The theory was that knitters could complete a garment from a single skein without having to purchase additional yarn, thus eliminating the need for a dye lot. Over the years I adjusted yardage and patterns to account for differences in individual tension, ensuring that there was 10% more yarn than what was actually needed.

The skein-specific patterns offered several advantages. Projects were inexpensive because they were designed for a specific amount of yarn, so there was no need to buy an additional skein for what might amount to a few rows but would double the cost of the project. Even without the use of large needles, these small projects held the knitter's interest and knit quickly. They were also portable, so that time spent idly waiting at the dentist's office or riding in the car or subway could be spent knitting.

Eventually, I learned to create dye lots and produced bags of similarly painted yarn. But the patterns that consumed just one hank remained popular with customers. I learned that many knitters found ways to reuse the same favorite pattern with many different yarns purchased from a variety of companies and venues. Some knitters admitted that they actually prowled yarn stores and the Internet looking for single skeins because they enjoyed the challenge of creating a project from one skein alone or in combination with other yarns.

Here you will discover more than 25 projects ranging in difficulty from beginner to intermediate and containing tips for best managing the yardage at hand. The projects are grouped into sections according to yarn weight, and each section offers a variety of projects that use a wide range of fibers, from wools to cottons to synthetics.

Specific yardage is given for each project so that you may accurately choose which yarn or combination of yarns will complete any garment before you begin. As long as you have the correct weight of yarn (for example, fingering weight) and can achieve gauge, feel free to experiment further with other combinations of yarns and projects outside the scope of this book. Although these patterns are designed for one skein, it is not necessary to use just one. If your yarn yardage is less than what is listed for the project, I encourage you to combine several single skeins. If your skein has more yardage than needed, just use a partial skein. You'll find that you can produce many different looks with these simple patterns just by choosing different kinds of yarns each time. Remember that inside every orphan is a one-hank wonder just waiting for you to discover its designer appeal.

This garment is made from one skein of yarn.

Common YARN WEIGHTS and YARDAGES

FORTUNATELY for knitters everywhere, the Craft Yarn Council of America (CYCA) introduced a Standard Yarn-Weight System several years ago that knitting magazines and book publishers have adopted and modified for specific uses. This universal system places yarn into six distinct categories grouped by weight, and this information is often portrayed as a simple chart. Such charts include yarns ranging from the thinnest lace yarns to the bulkiest novelty blends and recommend a range of needle and crochet hook sizes to achieve a certain gauge.

It's important to remember that these are just guidelines. Loose knitters may have to drop a needle size to achieve gauge, and tight knitters may have to do the opposite. Also, these suggestions cover only stockinette-stitch swatches that yield knitted fabric with body and drape. If you're knitting a lacy stitch pattern, you might need larger needles than those listed. If you want a tightly woven fabric for socks, for example, you may need smaller needles.

For the purposes of this book, I have slightly modified the standard chart. I have included lace weight as the thinnest yarn because several of the projects use lace-weight yarn, and that information is not given in the standard chart. Another helpful category provided here is the number of yards a knitter can expect per ounce of yarn. This will aid you tremendously when you're attempting to gauge whether you have enough yarn to complete a given project. To simplify things, the super-bulky yarn information has been deleted from the chart because none of the projects use yarn thicker than bulky.

STANDARD YARN-WEIGHT SYSTEM (Slightly Modified)

Yarn-Weight Symbol and Category Names	0 Lace	1 Super fine	2 Fine	3 Light	4 Medium	5 Bulky
Types of Yarns in Category	Lace	Sock, Fingering, Baby	Sport, Baby	DK, Light Worsted	Worsted, Afghan, Aran	Chunky, Craft, Rug
Knit Gauge Ranges in Stockinette Stitch to 4"	27 to 32 sts	27 to 32 sts	23 to 26 sts	21 to 24 sts	16 to 20 sts	12 to 15 sts
Recommended Needle in Metric Size Range	2 to 3.25 mm	2.25 to 3.25 mm	3.25 to 3.75 mm	3.75 to 4.5 mm	4.5 to 5.5 mm	5.5 to 8 mm
Recommended Needle in U.S. Size Range	0 to 3	1 to 3	3 to 5	5 to 7	7 to 9	9 to 11
Approximate Yardage per Ounce	300	100 to 150	80 to 100	70 to 90	50 to 75	35 to 50

Following are general descriptions of the yarns used and what to expect. To assist you further, strands of all yarns are shown actual size.

LACE

Lace-weight yarns

Lace-weight yarn shown actual size

Lace-weight yarn is often called super fine and is typically thinner than sock or fingering yarn. Depending on your project, you will find that needle sizes range from 0 to 3, and projects with large areas of lace patterning may require even larger needles. Skeins typically come in the 1.75-ounce size, and you can expect about 300 yards per ounce. Most scarf patterns call for 300 to 500 yards, and shawls call for 700 to 900 yards.

FINGERING

Fingering-weight yarn

Fingering-weight yarn shown actual size

Some publications place fingering-weight yarn in the super-fine category and others place it in the fine category. I consider it to be fine yarn and would use a needle size range of 2 to 4 for socks. If you're knitting something lacy like the Glitter Alpaca

Scarves on page 35, you will need larger needles to create simple lacy stitch patterns and allow the alpaca to loft. Skeins typically come in the 4-ounce size and you can expect about 100 to 150 yards per ounce. Most scarf patterns call for 200 to 250 yards, and socks call for 350 to 500 yards, depending on size.

SPORT AND DOUBLE KNITTING (DK)

Sport-weight and DK-weight yarn

Sport-weight yarn shown actual size

In this book I have combined sport and DK yarns into the same category. Sport-weight yarn is lighter than DK and can be knit with a smaller needle, but my experience is that larger needles show the yarn to its best advantage, especially if the yarn is one that lofts easily or is a novelty or bouclé [boo-CLAY], such as Baby Loop Mohair used in the Circles Shawl on page 49. Even DK yarn, which is slightly heavier than sport, is considered a light yarn, and for either one I recommend a size 5 to 7 needle.

Sport and DK skeins typically come in the 4-ounce size, and knitters often purchase multiple hanks to complete a garment. Sport yarns yield about 80 to 100 yards per ounce, depending on content and yarn construction, while DK yarns yield slightly less, about 70 to 90 yards per ounce. A 4-ounce skein of sport or DK-weight yarn can be enough to knit a hat or pair of mittens. For socks, allow about 400 yards of sport or about 300 yards of DK. You will use 8 ounces of either sport or DK to complete a large shawl.

WORSTED

Worsted-weight yarn

Worsted-weight yarn shown actual size

Worsted-weight is the most common yarn in the knitting universe because of its versatility. It is considered medium-weight and is used to knit staple items such as hats, scarves, sweaters, and afghans. Skeins are usually 4 ounces, and yardage ranges from 50 to 75 yards per ounce. Needle size ranges from 6 to 8, and sometimes 9, for yarn we might call heavy worsted or light bulky. Most patterns call for several skeins of yarn, and it is unlikely that many projects can be completed from just one skein, unless the project is a simple hat or a child's item.

BULKY

Bulky-weight yarn

Bulky-weight yarn shown actual size

What I call bulky yarn is considered chunky weight and usually comes in skeins weighing 4 to 8 ounces. In department stores, it is often called craft or rug yarn and is composed of synthetic fiber. Multiple skeins are required to knit anything larger than a hat, and yardage per ounce falls between 35 and 50 yards. I recommend a size 9 to 11 needle. A larger needle would be used for special effects.

PROJECTS WITH LACE-WEIGHT YARNS

Lace-weight yarn can be deceptive. The yarn appears so thin that knitters sometimes wear reading glasses or magnifiers to cast on, and the yarn looks so frail that knitters hesitate to knit firmly lest the yarn fray or fall away to nothing. But don't let the size of a diminutive skein fool you. Lace-weight yarn generally offers 475 yards per hank, and the often-used open lacy stitches make the yarn go even farther. The fact that many lace projects are finished by wetting the garment and stretching it with pins is testimony to the strength of the yarn as well as its elasticity. One drawback of knitting with lace yarns is that small needles and a myriad of stitches are the norm.

Examples of lace-weight yarns

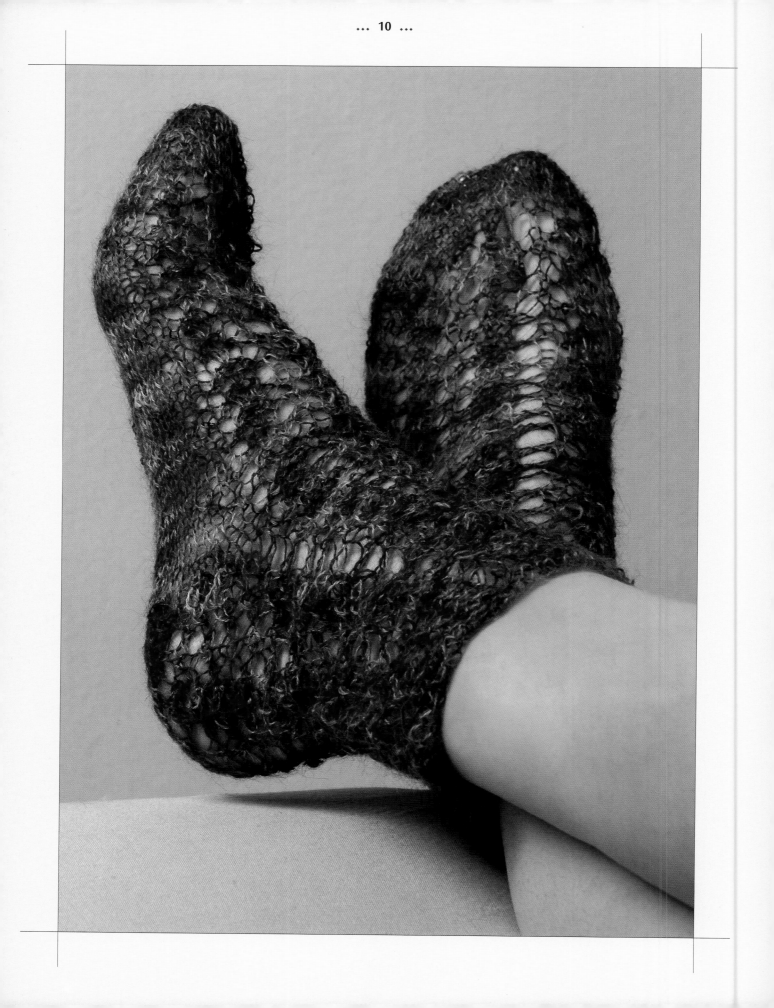

Suri Lace SOCKS *By Judy Sumner*

Judy is a well-known and innovative sock designer, and over the years we have collaborated on many projects. One of my favorites was a pair of boudoir socks called Sheer Delight that she designed using lace-weight cashmere. Impractical for everyday use, they were ideal for wearing to bed in cold weather. Judy's latest design is this pair of delicate bed socks knit from just one skein of a soft and luscious alpaca yarn called Suri Lace.

Because it is easy to drop stitches when working with this fine yarn (and then hard to pick them back up in the lace pattern), Judy advises knitters to knit tightly and avoid metal needles; they tend to be too slippery for this yarn. These lace socks are worth the effort, however, because they have a lot of give and will shape themselves to your feet, keeping them toasty warm.

If you don't feel like casting on hundreds of stitches or involving yourself with fancy patterning, try these lace socks for a refreshing change. Suri Lace Socks are shown in the colorway Dusk.

Skill Level: Intermediate

Size: One size fits adult woman

Gauge: 7 sts and 8 rows =1" in St st on size 3 needles

MATERIALS

~1 hank of Suri Alpaca Lace from Cherry Tree Hill (100% Suri alpaca; 442 yds; 50 g) in color Dusk 🔟

~Size 3 and 4 double-pointed needles, set of 5 each

~Size F/5 (4 mm) crochet hook

~Tapestry needle

LACE PATTERN

For lace patt, you may follow chart below right or follow rnds 1–4 here.

Rnds 1 and 3: Knit.

Rnd 2: YO, skp, K1, K2tog, YO, K1.

Rnd 4: K1, YO, sk2p, YO, K2.

Rep rnds 1–4 for patt.

CUFF

Loosely CO 48 sts onto 4 size 4 dpns (12 sts per needle), pm, join in the round, being careful not to twist sts, and mark beg of rnd.

Row 1: Knit.

Row 2: Purl.

Rows 3 and 4: Rep rows 1 and 2.

Change to size 3 needles and beg lace patt. When work measures 6" from beg, complete row 4 and beg heel flap.

DIVIDE FOR HEEL

Turn work. Purl across 12 sts on this needle and 12 sts on next needle. You now have 24 sts on one needle for heel flap. Turn work and cont lace patt on these 24 sts, purling rows 1 and 3 rather than knitting them. Work total of 4 lace patt reps and purl back.

TURN HEEL

Row 1: Sl 1, K13, skp, K1, turn.

Row 2: Sl 1, P5, P2tog, P1, turn.

Row 3: Sl 1, K6, skp, K1, turn.

Row 4: Sl 1, P7, P2tog, P1, turn.

Cont in this manner, working 1 more st before dec on each row until 14 sts rem.

Next row: Knit.

GUSSET

With crochet hook, pick up 8 sts along side of heel flap. Work patt across 2 instep needles. With crochet hook, pick up 8 sts along other side of heel flap. Divide heel sts between what are now needles 1 and 4. Instep needles are 2 and 3. This is now beg of rnd.

Rnd 1: Knit.

Rnd 2: On needle 1, knit to last 3 sts, skp, K1.

On needles 2 and 3, work lace patt.

On needle 4, K1, K2tog, knit rem sts.

Rnd 3: On needles 1 and 4, knit. On needles 2 and 3, work patt.

Rep rnds 2 and 3 until heel needles (1 and 4) have 12 sts each.

FOOT

Work around as est until foot length is 1½" less than desired length from back of heel.

TOE

Rnd 1: On needle 1, work to last 3 sts, skp, K1.

On needle 2, K1, K2tog, knit to end.

On needle 3, knit to last 3 sts, skp, K1.

On needle 4, K1, K2tog, knit to end.

Rnd 2: Knit.

Rep rnds 1 and 2 until 5 sts rem on each needle. Referring to "Kitchener Stitch" on page 107, combine sts from needles 1 and 4 onto one needle and sts from needles 2 and 3 onto one needle and graft toe.

FINISHING

It is not necessary to block these socks. However, if blocking is desired, wet socks in warm water and shape them on towel or other blocking surface and let dry.

Lace pattern

Key

☐	K
○	YO
⟋	sl 1, K1, psso
⟍	K2 tog
⟋⟍	sl 1, K2 tog, psso

Gypsy Rose SCARF

By Barbara Venishnick

In general, scarves are always a good project for one skein of yarn because the length and width are arbitrary and you can make it short, long, narrow, or wide, depending on the amount of yarn available, without changing the usefulness of the finished garment. If short yardage is known at the outset of a project, narrow the scarf and gain length by eliminating one pattern repeat. If the short yardage is not discovered until you are nearing the end of a project, you can make a shorter scarf by binding off when the end is near.

One plus for this scarf is the absence of fringe, so there is no need to reserve yarn for it. Leave just enough yarn to bind off. The thinner Suri is best knit with an inverse-tip needle that scoops the yarn up easily. Bryspun needles do this and are excellent for lacework with fine yarns.

Gypsy Rose Scarf is shown knit with Possum Lace (above left) and also with Suri Lace (above right).

Skill Level: Easy
Finished Size: 6" x 67" after blocking
Gauge: 33 sts and 28 rows = 4" in herringbone patt

MATERIALS

~1 hank of Suri Lace from Cherry Tree Hill (100% Suri alpaca; 442 yds; 50 g) in color Gypsy Rose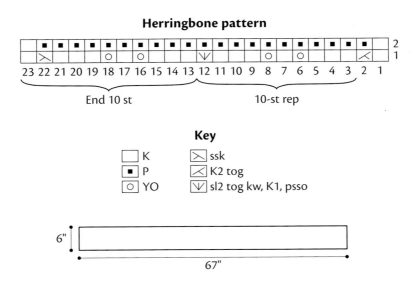

~Size 3 needles

HERRINGBONE PATTERN

For herringbone patt, you may follow chart below or follow rows 1 and 2 here.

Row 1 (RS): K1, K2tog, *K3, YO, K1, YO, K3, sl 2 sts tog as if to K2tog, K1, pass 2 sl sts over K1 st; rep from * to last 10 sts, K3, YO, K1, YO, K3, ssk, K1.

Row 2: K1, purl to last st, K1.

Rep rows 1 and 2 for patt.

SCARF

CO 63 sts. Knit 2 rows.

Work patt until piece measures 62" or desired length, ending with row 2 of patt. Purl 2 rows. With RS facing you, BO all sts pw. Weave in loose ends. Block to measurements.

Herringbone pattern

```
 2
 1
23 22 21 20 19 18 17 16 15 14 13 12 11 10 9 8 7 6 5 4 3 2 1
      End 10 st                    10-st rep
```

Key

☐	K	⊠	ssk
▪	P	⊿	K2 tog
○	YO	⩒	sl2 tog kw, K1, psso

6"

67"

Cascade CAPELET *By Kristin Omdahl*

This capelet with a falling-leaf motif not only showcases the lustrous silk but also makes the cape look longer than it is, due to the falling leaves. A wavy scalloped border also contributes to this optical illusion.

One advantage to lace knitting is that it blocks to a much larger size than you might guess. Using a lace stitch is a way to maximize 1,000 yards of silk. For the garter neckband, placket, and bottom border, slipping the first stitch of every row ensures a good-looking finished edge with no need for additional treatment.

Because it is a shaped garment knit from the top down, if you do run short of yarn you could always stop short of your desired length.

The falling-leaf motif combined with an earth-toned colorway is a perfect fit for this silk capelet. Cascade Capelet is knit with Cascade Lace and shown in the colorway Serengeti.

Skill Level: Intermediate

Finished Length: 15"

Gauge: 5 sts and 6 rows = 1" in patt st after blocking

MATERIALS

~1 hank of Cascade Lace from Cherry Tree Hill (100% silk; 1,000 yds; 150 g) in color Serengeti 🔟

~29" size 5 circular needle

~29" size 11 needle for loose BO

~2 stitch markers

~5 buttons, ¾" diameter

~Sewing needle and thread for buttons

Note: The button plackets are worked over the first and last 5 stitches of each row throughout, always slipping the first stitch in each row. Buttonholes are worked in neckband rows 5 and 6 and capelet rows 5 and 6, 15–16, 25–26, and 35–36.

NECKBAND

Note: Slip markers as they appear in the rows.

Using size 5 needle, CO 5 sts, pm, CO 100 sts, pm, CO 5 sts—110 sts.

Row 1: Sl 1, K4, knit to next marker, K5.

Rows 2–4: Rep row 1.

Row 5: Sl 1, K1, YO twice, sk2p, knit to next marker, K5.

Row 6: Sl 1, K4, knit to next marker, K1, K1f&b of double YO from last row, K2.

Rows 7–9: Rep row 1.

Row 10: Sl 1, K4, (K1f&b, K4) 20 times, K5—130 sts.

Row 11: Sl 1, K4, purl to next marker, K5.

CAPELET

Row 1: Sl 1, K4, (K1, YO, K1, YO, K1, skp, K9, K2tog, K1, YO, K1, YO, K2) 6 times, K5—142 sts.

Row 2: Sl 1, K4, purl to next marker, K5.

Row 3: Sl 1, K4, (K2, YO, K1, YO, K2, skp, K7, K2tog, K2, YO, K1, YO, K3) 6 times, K5—154 sts.

Row 4: Rep row 2.

Row 5: Sl 1, K1, YO twice, sk2p, (K3, YO, K1, YO, K3, skp, K5, K2tog, K3, YO, K1, YO, K4) 6 times, K5—166 sts.

Row 6: Sl 1, K4, purl to next marker, K1, K1f&b of double YO from last row, K2.

Row 7: Sl 1, K4, (K4, YO, K1, YO, K4, skp, K3, K2tog, K4, YO, K1, YO, K5) 6 times, K5—178 sts.

Rows 8, 10, 12, and 14: Rep row 2.

Row 9: Sl 1, K4, (YO, K5, YO, K1, YO, K5, skp, K1, K2tog, K5, YO, K1, YO, K5, YO, K1) 6 times, K5—202 sts.

Row 11: Sl 1, K4, (YO, K1, YO, K13, YO, sk2p, YO, K13 [YO, K1] twice) 6 times, K5—226 sts.

Row 13: Sl 1, K4, (K1, [YO, K1, YO, K1, skp, K9, K2tog, K1] twice, YO, K1, YO, K2) 6 times, K5—238 sts.

Row 15: Sl 1, K1, YO twice, sk2p, (K2, [YO, K1, YO, K2, skp, K7, K2tog, K2] twice, YO, K1, YO, K3) 6 times, K5—250 sts.

Row 16: Rep row 6.

Row 17: Sl 1, K4, (K3, [YO, K1, YO, K3, skp, K5, K2tog, K3] twice, YO, K1, YO, K4) 6 times, K5—262 sts.

Rows 18, 20, 22, and 24: Rep row 2.

Row 19: Sl 1, K4, (K4, [YO, K1, YO, K4, skp, K3, K2tog, K4] twice, YO, K1, YO, K5) 6 times, K5—274 sts.

Row 21: Sl 1, K4, (YO, K5, [YO, K1, YO, K5, skp, K1, K2tog, K5] twice, YO, K1, YO, K5, YO, K1) 6 times, K5—298 sts.

Row 23: Sl 1, K4, (YO, K1, YO, K6, [K7, YO, sk2p, YO, K6] twice, K7, [YO, K1] twice) 6 times, K5—322 sts.

Row 25: Sl 1, K1, YO twice, sk2p, (K1, [YO, K1, YO, K1, skp, K9, K2tog, K1] 3 times, YO, K1, YO, K2) 6 times, K5—334 sts.

Row 26: Rep row 6.

Row 27: Sl 1, K4, (K2, [YO, K1, YO, K2, skp, K7, K2tog, K2] 3 times, YO, K1, YO, K3) 6 times, K5—346 sts.

Rows 28, 30, 32, and 34: Rep row 2.

Row 29: Sl 1, K4, (K3, [YO, K1, YO, K3, skp, K5, K2tog, K3] 3 times, YO, K1, YO, K4) 6 times, K5—358 sts.

Row 31: Sl 1, K4, (K4, [YO, K1, YO, K4, skp, K3, K2tog, K4] 3 times, YO, K1, YO, K5) 6 times, K5—370 sts.

Row 33: Sl 1, K4, (YO, K5, [YO, K1, YO, K5, skp, K1, K2tog, K5] 3 times, YO, K1, YO, K5, YO, K1) 6 times, K5—394 sts.

Row 35: Sl 1, K1, YO twice, sk2p, (YO, K1, YO, K6, [K7, YO, sk2p, YO, K6] 3 times, K7, [YO, K1] twice) 6 times, K5—418 sts.

Row 36: Rep row 6.

Row 37: Sl 1, K4, (K1, [YO, K1, YO, K1, skp, K9, K2tog, K1] 4 times, YO, K1, YO, K2) 6 times, K5—430 sts.

Rows 38, 40, 42, 44, 46, 48, 50, 52, 54, and 56: Rep row 2.

Row 39: Sl 1, K4, (K2, [YO, K1, YO, K2, skp, K7, K2tog, K2] 4 times, YO, K1, YO, K3) 6 times, K5—442 sts.

Row 41: Sl 1, K4, (K3, [YO, K1, YO, K3, skp, K5, K2tog, K3] 4 times, YO, K1, YO, K4) 6 times, K5—454 sts.

Row 43: Sl 1, K4, (K4, [YO, K1, YO, K4, skp, K3, K2tog, K4] 4 times, YO, K1, YO, K5) 6 times, K5—466 sts.

Row 45: Sl 1, K4, (YO, K5, [YO, K1, YO, K5, skp, K1, K2tog, K5] 4 times, YO, K1, YO, K5, YO, K1) 6 times, K5—490 sts.

Row 47: Sl 1, K4, (YO, K1, YO, K6, [K7, YO, sk2p, YO, K6] 4 times, K7, [YO, K1] twice) 6 times, K5—514 sts.

Row 49: Sl 1, K4, ([YO, skp, K1, YO, skp, K9, K2tog] 5 times, YO, skp, K1, YO, K1) 6 times, K5—490 sts.

Row 51: Sl 1, K4, ([YO, skp, K1, YO, K1, YO, skp, K7, K2tog] 5 times, YO, skp, K1, YO, K1, YO, K1) 6 times, K5—502 sts.

Row 53: Sl 1, K4, (YO, skp, [K1, YO] 4 times, skp, K5, K2tog) 5 times, YO, skp, [K1, YO] 4 times, K1) 6 times, K5—586 sts.

Row 55: Sl 1, K4, (YO, skp, [K1, YO] 8 times, skp, K3, K2tog) 5 times, YO, skp, [K1, YO] 8 times, K1) 6 times, K5—814 sts.

Row 57: Sl 1, K4, ([YO, skp] 10 times, K1, K2tog) 5 times, [YO, skp] 9 times, YO, K1) 6 times, K5—790 sts.

Row 58: Sl 1, K4, (K22, [P1, K21] 5 times) 6 times, K5—802 sts.

Rows 59–64: Knit.

With size 11 needle, BO loosely.

FINISHING

Wash, block, and let dry. Weave in loose ends. Using sewing needle and thread, sew buttons to opposite placket, directly in line with buttonholes.

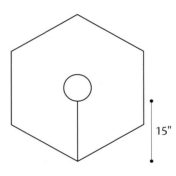

15"

Figure-Eight FANTASY SHAWL *By Kristin Omdahl*

Kristin's large figure-eight motif is bold enough to serve as a centerpiece. The center panel, containing the figure-eights and bordered on either side with wavy panels, will drape over a 4" x 6" table. Kristin resorted to her trusty digital scale to ensure that she allocated enough yarn for each section. To begin, she knit one figure-eight motif, washed and blocked it, and then weighed and measured it. Because she used a lacy openwork stitch pattern, the size grew dramatically after blocking.

Once Kristin decided how many motifs she would need to knit, she reserved that amount of yarn. The remainder of the yarn she divided in half for the two side panels. The length of the side panels is arbitrary. As long as you allocate equal amounts of yarn for each side panel, Kristin advises you to just keep knitting until you only have enough to bind off; the side panels will look symmetrical regardless of length.

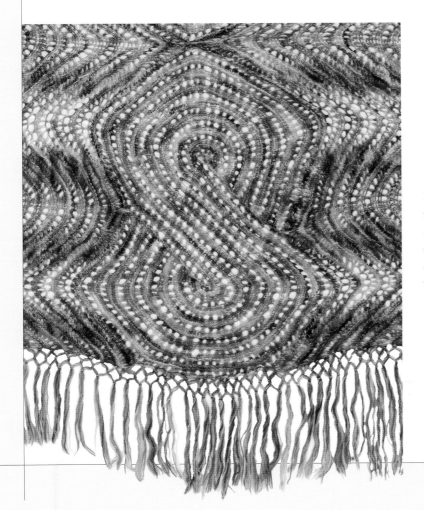

Figure-Eight Fantasy Shawl is knit with Merino Lace and shown in the colorway Monet with optional fringe. This large, versatile shawl doubles as a holiday tablecloth.

Skill Level: Intermediate
Finished Size: 72" x 40" without fringe
Motif: 24" x 14"
Panel: 72" x 13"
Gauge: 6 sts = 1" in patt st after blocking

MATERIALS

~1 hank of Merino Lace from Cherry Tree Hill (100%
   merino wool; 2,400 yds; 8 oz) in color Monet (**0**)
~36" size 7 circular needle
~Size 10½ needles for BO
~Size F/5 (4 mm) crochet hook
~7 stitch markers
~Tapestry needle
~Digital scale for dividing yarn (optional)

Note: To maximize yardage, use a digital scale to portion
off the yarn in the following amounts: 17 grams for each
motif, 70 grams per side panel, and 36 grams for fringe.
Each of these amounts include extra yarn for sewing motifs
and panels together later. If you don't have a digital scale,
don't worry. Make the motifs and side panels first, and then
divide the leftover yarn evenly for the fringe. Cast on stitches
very loosely.

MOTIFS (Make 3)

Using size 7 needles, (CO 24 sts, pm) 6 times, CO 20
sts, pm, CO 1 st—165 sts.

Note: Slip markers as they appear in the rows.

Row 1 (RS): (Knit, purl) 3 times all in first st, K20, (K1,
K2tog, K21) 6 times—164 sts.

Row 2: Purl.

Row 3: (K1f&b) 6 times, K20, (K3, K2tog, K18) 6 times.

Row 4: P1, (YO, P2tog) to last st, P1.

Row 5: (K1, K1f&b) 6 times, K20, (K5, K2tog, K15)
6 times.

Row 6: Knit.

Row 7: (K2, K1f&b) 6 times, K20, (K7, K2tog, K12)
6 times.

Row 8: Purl.

Row 9: (K1f&b, K3) 6 times, K20, (K9, K2tog, K9)
6 times.

Row 10: P1, (YO, P2tog) to last st, P1.

Row 11: (K2, K1f&b, K2) 6 times, K20, (K1, K2tog, K16)
6 times.

Row 12: Knit.

Row 13: (K5, K1f&b) 6 times, K20, (K5, K2tog, K11) 6
times.

Row 14: Purl.

Row 15: (K1f&b, K6) 6 times, K20, (K15, K2tog) 6
times.

Row 16: P1, (YO, P2tog) to last st, P1.

Row 17: (K3, K1f&b, K4) 6 times, K20, (K8, K2tog, K6)
6 times.

Row 18: Knit.

Row 19: (K1, K1f&b, K7) 6 times, K20, (K1, K2tog,
K12) 6 times.

Row 20: Purl.

Row 21: (K5, K1f&b, K4) 6 times, K20, (K5, K2tog, K7)
6 times.

Row 22: P1, (YO, P2tog) to last st, P1.

Row 23: (K7, K1f&b, K3) 6 times, K20, (K7, K2tog, K4)
6 times.

Row 24: Knit.

Row 25: (K9, K1f&b, K2) 6 times, K20, (K9, K2tog, K1)
6 times.

Row 26: Purl.

Row 27: (K11, K1f&b, K1) 6 times, K20, (K1, K2tog,
K8) 6 times.

Row 28: P1, (YO, P2tog) to last st, P1.

Row 29: (K13, K1f&b) 6 times, K20, (K3, K2tog, K5) 6
times.

Row 30: Knit.

Row 31: (K1, K1f&b, K13) 6 times, K20, (K5, K2tog,
K2) 6 times.

Row 32: Purl.

Row 33: (K3, K1f&b, K12) 6 times, K20, (K6, K2tog) 6
times.

Row 34: P1, (YO, P2tog) to last st, P1.

Row 35: (K5, K1f&b, K11) 6 times, K20, (K1, K2tog,
K4) 6 times.

Row 36: Knit.

Row 37: (K7, K1f&b, K10) 6 times, K20, (K2, K2tog,
K2) 6 times.

Row 38: Purl.

Row 39: (K9, K1f&b, K9) 6 times, K20, (K3, K2tog) 6 times.

Row 40: P1, (YO, P2tog) to last st, P1.

Row 41: (K11, K1f&b, K8) 6 times, K20, (K2, K2tog) 6 times.

Row 42: Knit.

Row 43: (K13, K1f&b, K7) 6 times, K20, (K2tog, K1) 6 times.

Row 44: Purl.

Row 45: (K1, K1f&b, K20) 6 times, K20, (K2tog) 6 times.

Row 46: P1, (YO, P2tog) to last st, P1.

Row 47: (K4, K1f&b, K18) 6 times, remove marker, K20, sl 3 sts pw, K3tog, p3sso.

With 10½ needles, BO loosely.

Block motifs to 24" x 14". Using tapestry needle and yarn, sew seams per diagram to form figure eights. Set motifs aside.

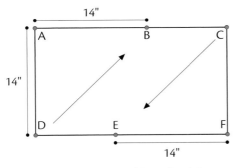

Fold D to B, matching edge AD to edge AB. Sew AD along AB.

Fold C to E, matching edge CF to edge EF. Sew CF along EF.

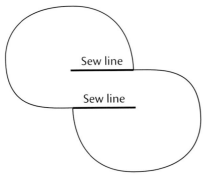

Figure-eight motif after sewing

SIDE PANELS (Make 2)

(CO 72 sts, pm) 5 times, CO 72 sts—432 sts.

Note: Slip markers as they appear in the rows.

Row 1 (RS): Knit.

Row 2: Purl.

Row 3: K1, (YO, K2tog) across.

Row 4: Purl.

Row 5: (K2tog 12 times, [K1, YO] 24 times, ssk 12 times) 6 times.

Row 6: Knit across.

Rows 7–78: Work rows 1–6 another 11 times or until 2 g of yarn rem.

Use crochet BO to finish edge. With crochet hook, *sl 3 sts pw onto crochet hook, YO and draw loop through all 3 sts, ch 9, rep from * to last 3 sts, sl 3 sts pw onto hook, YO and draw loop through all 3 sts. Fasten off and weave in ends.

FINISHING

Block each panel to 72" x 13". Using tapestry needle and yarn, sew CO edge of side panels to motifs according to diagram. Ripple points for each panel shown as 1, 3, 5 and 7 will touch each other at center of motifs. Ease in fullness between ripple points.

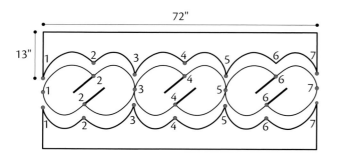

Cut fringe yarn into 18"-long pieces. Attach to short sides in groups of 6. See "Fringe" on page 108. Trim fringe for an even edge.

Optional Fringe

After attaching fringe to short sides and before trimming, you can make fringe decorative by tying 2 rows of knots.

Knot row 1: Leave 6 strands of first fringe free. Using other 6 strands of first fringe and 6 strands from adjacent fringe, tie knot ½" from slipknot. Rep across side, using 6 strands from each adjacent fringe to tie knots. Leave rem 6 strands of last fringe free.

Knot row 2: Using 6 free strands of fringe from first knot row and 6 strands from adjacent fringe, knot ½" from last row of knots. Rep across side, using 6 strands from each adjacent fringe to tie knots. Last knot should include last 6 free strands from first knot row. Trim fringe for even edge.

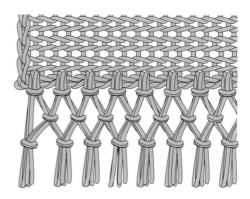

FUN WITH FINGERING-WEIGHT YARNS

Most knitters consider fingering-weight yarn thin, and many—including myself—rarely venture to ply their needles with any smaller-diameter fiber. Commonly knit for socks, fingering yarn is actually more versatile than you might imagine and is often used for hats, scarves, gloves, baby items, and lace projects. Because it yields high yardage per ounce, fingering weight can be used with confidence in garter stitch and other patterning that seems to consume yarn. Even so, it is wise to have a contingency plan if you happen to run short.

A variety of fingering-weight yarns

Pocket PURSE *By Sharon Mooney*

Handy for change and small treats such as penny candy, this purse is small enough to keep in a jacket pocket or slip into a pocketbook. Sharon thought it would be a great project for using up leftover Supersock, which comes in 4-ounce skeins and has 420 yards. Several pocket purses can be knit from one skein—or you may decide to knit a pair of socks first, and then make a pocket purse from the leftovers.

Garter stitch gives the purse body, shape, and durability, and because there is no pattern repeat to think about, this purse can be easily made smaller or larger depending on the amount of yarn available. If the yardage runs short, you can make the purse narrower or shorter and it will still work as a change purse, but you might have to leave out the penny candy.

Pocket Purse is knit with Supersock and shown in the colorway Winterberry. The Pocket Purse can be used as a bag on its own, but it's also small enough to fit into the pocket of a purse.

Skill Level: Intermediate

Finished Size: 5½" wide x 3" high with flap down

Gauge: 7 sts and 15 rows (8 ridges) = 1" in garter st

MATERIALS

~½ hank of Supersock from Cherry Tree Hill (100% merino wool; 210 yds; 2 oz) in color Winterberry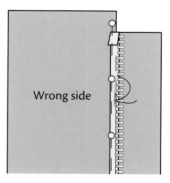

~Size 2 needles

~Tapestry needle

~7" dark purple plastic zipper

~Straight pins

~Sewing needle and thread for zipper

~3" x 3" piece of cardboard

FLAP

CO 35 sts.

Row 1 (RS): K1, (P1, K1) to end.

Rows 2–3: P1, (K1, P1) to end.

Row 4: K1, (P1, K1) to end.

Rows 5–12: Rep rows 1–4 twice.

BAG

Row 13: CO 2 sts, knit to end—37 sts.

Row 14: CO 2 sts, knit to end—39 sts.

Knit every row until piece measures 7" from beg.

BO and cut yarn end to 6".

FINISHING

With tapestry needle, weave in all loose ends. Cut off excess yarn. Block if necessary.

Fold bag in half, WS tog, with BO edge lining up with row 13. Thread needle with length of yarn and use mattress st to close both side seams. Weave in ends.

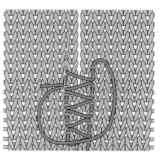

Pull tight every inch or so.

Zipper

1. Using tapestry needle and yarn, make zipper stop 5½" from top teeth of zipper by wrapping teeth 3 to 4 times tightly and securing. Cut zipper ½" below zipper stop you just made.

2. Fold purse WS out. Fold down zipper top tabs to WS of zipper and pin in place. Align and pin one side of open zipper, WS up, in place on WS of purse. Teeth of zipper will fall across row that separates flap from garter sts of purse.

3. Using sewing needle and thread, sew zipper in place close to but below teeth with small backstitches.

4. Turn purse RS out. Arrange seams around ends of zipper and pin in place. Bring BO edge up to zipper teeth on the unsewn edge of the zipper, but be careful not to cover teeth. Sew in place with small backstitches. Rep steps 2–4 for other side of zipper.

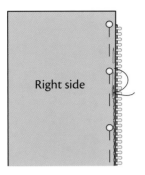

Tassel

1. Wrap yarn around cardboard 30 times. Cut yarn at one edge of cardboard.

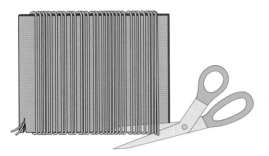

2. Lay center of these strands perpendicularly across another 2 strands of 6"-long yarn. Wrap 2 strands around bundle of strands and tie tightly.

3. Fold bundle of strands in half at tied end. Take another 6"-long strand of yarn and wrap it around top of folded bundle to make tassel.

4. Thread tapestry needle with ends of first 2 strands (used to tie all strands tog) and push needle through hole in zipper tab. Pull tight to bring tassel up to zipper tab. Push needle down through head of tassel and secure with few little sts. Bury ends of yarn inside tassel head and clip off any excess yarn. Trim ends of tassel to make it even.

Potluck SUPERSOCKS *By Cheryl Potter*

Color families are groups of similar dyes applied at whim from the color combinations left over after a day in the dye kitchen—the luck of the pot! Potluck dye skeins are painted individually, in no colorway or dye lot. Because each resultant skein cannot be duplicated, completing a project from one skein of potluck is essential. Potluck Supersocks is a perfect project, because the freer use of color and whimsical shading in the potluck-dye process lends itself to bright socks.

Unlike most careful sock knitters, I did not divide my yarn in half, nor did I start from the toe up. To keep the socks looking somewhat the same, and to even the progression should I run out of yarn, I knit the socks in consecutive sections with matching sets of double-pointed needles. I knit one cuff and then the other, then one heel flap and then the other, continuing this alternation with the gusset and toe shaping until the socks were finished. I used this method to develop the pattern; however, to be sure you have enough yarn for both socks, divide the yarn in half before beginning.

Potluck Supersocks are shown in color family Brights.

Getting the Most out of Your Yarn

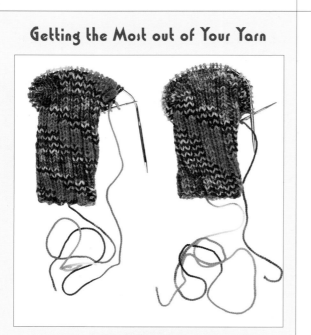

Knitting socks in consecutive sections will keep them looking similar even with potluck yarn.

If yardage runs short, try knitting heels and toes in a contrasting yarn.

Skill Level: Intermediate

Size: One size fits adult woman

Gauge: 5½ sts = 1" in St st

MATERIALS

~1 hank of Supersock from Cherry Tree Hill (100% superwash merino wool; 420 yds; 4 oz) in color Brights (1)

~Scrap of Supersock (approx 50 yds) for contrasting heels and toes (optional)

~Size 3 double-pointed needles, set of 4

~Tapestry needle

Note: *Sl sts pw, except for ssk.*

CUFF

With one dpn, CO 48 sts. Divide evenly onto 3 needles (16 sts per needle). Join in the round, being careful not to twist sts, and mark beg of rnd.

*K2, P2, rep from * around. Work in K2, P2 ribbing for 5", stopping at marker, remove marker.

DIVIDE FOR HEEL

Note: *If you would like a contrasting heel, switch to a different color of Supersock at this point.*

Knit across next 24 sts (heel sts). Transfer sts around so that these 24 knit sts are on first needle and 12 sts are on each of other 2 needles. Work back and forth across first needle only as foll:

Row 1: *Sl 1, K1, rep from * across.

Row 2: Sl 1, purl across.

Rows 3–28: Rep rows 1 and 2.

Row 29: Rep row 1.

TURN HEEL

Row 1: P14, P2tog, P1, turn.

Row 2: Sl 1, K5, K2tog, K1, turn.

Row 3: Sl 1, purl to 1 st before last turn (you'll see small gap where last turn was), P2tog, P1, turn.

Row 4: Sl 1, knit to 1 st before last turn (look for gap), K2tog, K1, turn.

Rep rows 3 and 4 until all sts at ends are used up, ending with RS row. There will be 14 sts left.

GUSSET

Note: If you opted for contrasting heel, switch back to main color here.

Cont to work with same needle, PU 14 sts along side of heel (needle 1). Using new needle, work across sts on next 2 needles (needle 2) in rib patt as est. Using new needle, PU 14 sts along other side of heel, and cont knitting to center of heel sts: 7 sts (needle 3). There should now be 21 sts on needles 1 and 3, and 24 sts on needle 2. Center of heel is beg of rnd; needle 2 contains instep sts. Beg dec as foll:

Rnd 1: Knit on needles 1 and 3, work ribbing across needle 2 as est.

Rnd 2: On needle 1, knit to last 3 sts, K2tog, K1.

On needle 2, work ribbing patt.

On needle 3, K1, ssk, knit to end.

Rep rows 1 and 2 until there are 12 sts left on both needles 1 and 3. Needle 2 will rem at 24 sts since no dec take place there. You will now be back to original number of sts.

FOOT

Work even again, keeping needle 2 in rib patt as est, until length from back of heel is 2" less than desired length of finished sock. At this point you can slip sock on to see length. Only toenails should stick out.

TOE

Note: If you opted for the contrasting heel and toe, switch back to contrasting color.

Rearrange sts on needles, if necessary, so that there are now 12 sts on each of needles 1 and 3, and 24 sts on needle 2. Beg of rnd is still at center back of heel. Stop working instep sts in ribbing. Beg dec as foll:

Rnd 1: On needle 1, knit to last 3 sts, K2tog, K1.

On needle 2, K1, ssk, knit to last 3 sts, K2tog, K1.

On needle 3, K1, ssk, knit to end (center of heel).

Rnd 2: Knit on all 3 needles.

Rep rnds 1 and 2 until there are 12 sts left.

Transfer sts from needle 1 to needle 3. Referring to "Kitchener Stitch" on page 107, graft toe.

Make 2nd sock, counting rows to make sure it is same size.

Glitter Alpaca SCARVES *By JoAnne Turcotte*

JoAnne usually allows about 200 to 250 yards to knit a scarf. The Glitter Alpaca was thin and the yardage was on the short side, so she chose simple, lacy patterns to add length and width. This also created gaps where light could filter through to show off the glittery yarn. Large needles accompanied the lace pattern to create the largest possible surface area. These scarves have a short pattern stitch with just a 4-row repeat, so to maximize length, you can knit until just a few yards of yarn are left and bind off. If yardage runs short, just bind off earlier and remember that blocking can help increase the size because lace patterning can be stretched out a great deal.

These classic scarves use a short pattern stitch with a small number of rows per repeat to maximize length. Leafy Scarf top, Starry Scarf bottom.

Starry Scarf

Starry Scarf is shown in the colorway Foxy Lady, left.

Skill Level: Intermediate
Finished Size: 8" x 50" after blocking
Gauge: 4 sts =1" in patt st after blocking

MATERIALS

~1 hank of Glitter Alpaca from Cherry Tree Hill
(99% alpaca, 1% glitter; 222 yds; 50 g) in color
Foxy Lady **1**

~Size 8 needles

Scarf

Loosely CO 34 sts.

Rows 1 and 2: Knit.

Row 3 (RS): K4, *YO, K3, sl first of 3 knitted sts over other 2 knitted sts; rep from * to last 3 sts, K3.

Row 4: K3, purl to last 3 sts, K3.

Row 5: K3, *K3, sl first of 3 knitted sts over other 2 knitted sts, YO*, rep from * to last 4 sts, K4.

Row 6: K3, purl to last 3 sts, K3.

Rep rows 3–6 until 2 yds rem for BO, ending with WS row. Knit 2 rows. BO loosely. Weave in all ends. Block.

Leafy Scarf

Leafy Scarf is shown in the colorway Gypsy Rose, below.

Skill Level: Intermediate
Finished Size: 8" x 50" after blocking
Gauge: 4 sts =1" in patt st after blocking

MATERIALS

~1 hank of Glitter Alpaca from Cherry Tree Hill
(99% alpaca, 1% glitter; 222 yds; 50 g) in color
Gypsy Rose **1**

~Size 8 needles

Scarf

Loosely CO 33 sts.

Rows 1 and 2: Knit.

Row 3 (RS): K4, *YO, K2, ssk, K2tog, K2, YO, K1, rep from * to last 2 sts, K2.

Row 4: K2, purl to last 2 sts, K2.

Row 5: K3, *YO, K2, ssk, K2tog, K2, YO, K1, rep from * to last 3 sts, K3.

Row 6: K2, purl to last 2 sts, K2.

Rep rows 3–6 until 2 yds rem for BO, ending with WS row. Knit 2 rows. BO loosely. Weave in all ends. Block.

Beaded Glitter Alpaca HAT and GAUNTLETS

By Sharon Mooney

Sharon chose an easy, ribbed pattern with a repeating bead insertion as the focal point, turning the already glitzy Alpaca hat into a piece of wearable art. If yardage is running short, leave out one of the beading repeats just before the decreases to the crown. Keep trying the hat on to make sure it will still fit well, and then begin the decreases if necessary.

Gloves are not possible because of the yardage limitations of one skein, so Sharon decided on a gauntlet project that required just one size but featured a stretchy ribbing knit in the round to fit a variety of hands. The best place to make adjustments is in the wrist portion of the gauntlet where you can easily shorten the length by knitting fewer rows, making sure that both gauntlets are shortened by the same number of rows. You can also subtract length from the finger portion by knitting fewer rows in these sections. If you have to shorten the gauntlets, try them on before the knitting is finished to ensure a good fit.

The Beaded Glitter Alpaca Hat and Gauntlets are knit with Glitter Alpaca and shown in the colorway Winterberry. The Beaded Glitter Alpaca Hat and Gauntlets can each be knit from one skein.

Skill Level: Intermediate

Size: One size fits large child through adult woman

Gauge: 7½ sts = 1" in St st

Note: Beads are slid along the yarn and brought up to the stitches as needed, which is indicated by "PB." Keep beads on the right side of the work.

MATERIALS FOR HAT

~1 hank of Glitter Alpaca (99% alpaca, 1% glitter; 222 yds; 50 g) in color Winterberry (**1**)

~16" size 2 circular needle

~Size 2 double-pointed needles, set of 4

~462 Mill Hill 6/0 (3.75 mm) beads in color 16609 Black

~Stitch marker

~Beading needle

~Tapestry needle

INSTRUCTIONS FOR HAT

Hat Rim

Using beading needle, string 462 beads onto yarn.

Using circular needle, CO 165 sts and join into rnd. Pm on needle to indicate beg of rnd. Change to dpn when necessary.

Rnds 1 and 2: *K3, P2, rep from * to end.

Rnd 3: *K1, yf, sl 1, PB, yb, K1, P2, rep from * to end.

Rnds 4 and 5: *K3, P2, rep from * to end.

Rnds 6–50: Work rows 1–5 another 9 times.

Crown Decrease

Rnd 1: *K3, P2, K3, P2, K3, P2tog, rep from * to end—154 sts.

Rnd 2: *K3, P2, K3, P2, K3, P1, rep from * to end.

Rnd 3: *K1, yf, sl 1, PB, yb, K1, P2, K1, yf, sl 1, PB, yb, K1, P2, K1, yf, sl 1, PB, yb, K1, P1, rep from * to end.

Rnd 4: *K3, P2, K3, P2, K2, K2tog, rep from * to end—143 sts.

Rnds 5 and 6: *K3, P2, K3, P2, K3, rep from * to end.

Rnd 7: *K3, P2, K3, P2, K1, K2tog, rep from * to end—132 sts.

Rnd 8: *K1, yf, sl 1, PB, yb, K1, P2, K1, yf, sl 1, PB, yb, K1, P2, K2, rep from * to end.

Rnd 9: *K3, P2, K3, P2, K2, rep from * to end.

Rnd 10: *K3, P2, K3, P2, K2tog, rep from * to end—121 sts.

Rnds 11 and 12: *K3, P2, K3, P2, K1, rep from * to end.

Rnd 13: *K1, yf, sl 1, PB, yb, K1, P2, K1, yf, sl 1, PB, yb, K1, P1, P2tog, rep from * to end—110 sts.

Rnds 14 and 15: *K3, P2, rep from * to end.

Rnd 16: *K3, P2, K3, P2tog, rep from * to end—99 sts.

Rnd 17: *K3, P2, K3, P1, rep from * to end.

Rnd 18: *K1, yf, sl 1, PB, yb, K1, P2, K1, yf, sl 1, PB, yb, K1, P1, rep from * to end.

Rnd 19: *K3, P2, K2, K2tog, rep from * to end—88 sts.

Rnds 20 and 21: *K3, P2, K3, rep from * to end.

Rnd 22: *K3, P2, K1, K2tog, rep from * to end—77 sts.

Rnd 23: *K1, yf, sl 1, PB, yb, K1, P2, K2, rep from * to end.

Rnd 24: *K3, P2, K2, rep from * to end.

Rnd 25: *K3, P2, K2tog, rep from * to end—66 sts.

Rnds 26 and 27: *K3, P2, K1, rep from * to end.

Rnd 28: *K1, yf, sl 1, PB, yb, K1, P1, P2tog, rep from * to end—55 sts.

Rnds 29 and 30: *K3, P2, rep from * to end.

Rnd 31: *K3, P2tog, rep from * to end—44 sts.

Rnd 32: *K3, P1, rep from * to end.

Rnd 33: *K1, yf, sl 1, PB, yb, K1, P1, rep from * to end.

Rnd 34: *K2, K2tog, rep from * to end—33 sts.

Rnd 35: Knit.

Rnd 36: *K1, K2tog, rep from * to end—22 sts.

Rnd 37: K2tog, rep to end—11 sts.

Finishing

Cut yarn end to 6" and thread through tapestry needle. Insert threaded needle through sts left on needles in same order as you would have knit them. Pull tight, closing top of hat, and push needle through to inside of hat. Weave in all loose ends. Cut off excess yarn. Block hat if necessary.

MATERIALS FOR GAUNTLETS

~1 hank of Glitter Alpaca (99% alpaca, 1% glitter; 222 yds; 50 g) in color Winterberry (1)

~Size 2 double-pointed needles, set of 4

~472 Mill Hill 6/0 (3.75 mm) beads in color 16609 Black

~Beading needle

~Stitch marker

~Tapestry needle

INSTRUCTIONS FOR GAUNTLETS (Make 2)

Using beading needle, string 236 beads onto yarn.

CO 70 sts and join into rnd. Pm to indicate beg of rnd.

Rnds 1 and 2: K3, P2 to end of rnd.

Rnd 3: (K1, yf, sl 1, PB, yb, K1, P2 to end of rnd.

Rnds 4 and 5: (K3, P2) to end of rnd.

Rnds 6–20: Work rnds 1–5 another 3 times.

Rnd 21: (K3, P2) 6 times, BO 10 sts, (K3, P2) to end of rnd.

Rnd 22: (K3, P2), rep to last 30 sts, CO 15 sts, (K3, P2) to end of rnd.

Rnds 23–25: Rep rnds 3–5.

Rnds 26–80: Work rnds 1–5 another 11 times.

BO in est patt. Cut yarn end to 6".

Finishing

Thread yarn end through tapestry needle and weave in all loose ends. Cut off excess yarn. Block gauntlets if necessary.

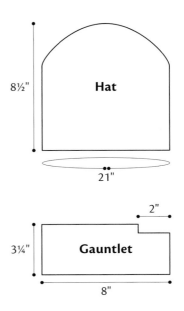

Cascade COVER-UP *By JoAnne Turcotte*

JoAnne created this easy and flattering openwork lace top that can be worn over a tank or bathing suit in the summer. Many patterns for fingering-weight yarn require high yardage in order to fit several sizes. But by adding an openwork pattern and top-down construction, this yarn's yardage is stretched to the max, allowing several sizes to be completed with just one skein.

JoAnne knit the front first, and instead of binding off, put it on a stitch holder while she knit the back. This way she could wait until the end to adjust the length. More length can easily be added or subtracted to use up more or less of the skein's available yardage. Or if the yardage runs short, just bind off earlier for a cropped cover-up. On the shown garment knit in the smallest size, a large portion of the skein was left over, so additional length could have been added to create a tunic top if desired.

This casual silk cover-up does not use an entire skein of Cascade, so it leaves lots of room to add length or width.

> ### Needle Choice for Lightweight Yarns
> Use needles with a well-defined point to help grab the K2tog and the P2tog of fingering or other lightweight yarns.

Skill Level: Intermediate
Sizes: 32–36 (38–42, 44–48)"
Finished Bust: 36 (42, 48) "
Finished Length: 21 (21, 20)"
Gauge: 14 sts = 4" in lace patt

MATERIALS

~1 hank of Cascade Fingering from Cherry Tree Hill (100% silk; 666 yds; 150 g) in color Monet **①**

~Size 8 needles

~Size 8 double-pointed needles for I-cord, set of 2

GARTER STITCH

Knit all rows.

LACE PATTERN

Row 1 (RS): (K2tog, YO) to end of section.

Row 2: (P2tog, YO) to end of section.

BACK AND FRONT (Make 2)

Cover-up is worked from top down.

Using single-point needles, CO 72 (82, 92) sts.

Rows 1–6: Knit.

Row 7 (RS): K5, work row 1 of lace patt across 62 (72, 82) sts, K5.

Row 8: K5, work row 2 of lace patt across 62 (72, 82) sts, K5.

Rep rows 7 and 8 until total armhole length is 8 (8½, 8½)", ending with WS row.

Shape Lower Body

Row 1 (RS): BO 4 sts, K1, work row 1 of lace patt across 62 (72, 82) sts, K5.

Row 2: BO 4 sts, K1, work row 2 of lace patt across 62 (72, 82) sts, K1.

Row 3: K1, work row 1 of lace patt across 62 (72, 82) sts, K1.

Row 4: K1, work row 2 of lace patt across 62 (72, 82) sts, K1.

Rep rows 3 and 4 until total length measures 20 (20, 19)".

Next 8 rows: Knit across all sts. BO.

With WS tog, sew side seams up to armholes.

Shoulders

Using dpns, make 6 pieces of 3-st I-cord, 12" long (see "I-Cord" on page 108). Leaving 8" to 10" at center open for neck, attach front and back tog at 3 evenly spaced points along each shoulder as shown in diagram below, tying each tog in bow. Weave in all ends.

Alternately, sew shoulders tog, leaving 10" open at center for neck.

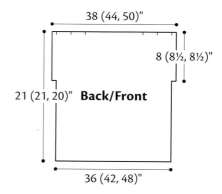

SPORT-WEIGHT AND DK-WEIGHT PROJECTS

I have combined sport and DK yarns into the same category because of their similar weights and yardage. These versatile yarns are often used in a wide variety of projects. Lighter sport weight is nice for socks and children's garments, should knitters desire to use a needle larger than a size 3, and also great for seasonal changes such as spring into summer or summer into fall. DK yarn is thicker than sport but slightly thinner than worsted weight and has become the norm for air-conditioned office wear. Knit into vests and sweaters or shawls and wraps, DK is an alternative to worsted weight for those who live in warm climates.

Various skeins of sport-weight and DK-weight yarns

Twister PONCHETTE *By Cheryl Potter*

I particularly like Twister yarn because it has a strand of superwash merino plied with the regular merino yarn so that a spiral of dark color is pulled along the skein. When Twister is knit, this soft, lightweight yarn creates an optical illusion of heavy tweed. My goal was to knit a lightweight poncho with the hand-loomed look of a Mexican serape.

I knew that running out of yarn was inevitable, so I cut all fringe first and set it aside for trim. If you desire a longer ponchette, you can do without the fringe or fringe it with coordinating scrap yarn from your stash. Knitting the ponchette from the top down means that there is no need to divide the yarn in half because you knit both front and back together, and you can shape as you go, which conserves yarn. When you begin to run out of yarn, you can start binding off at the sides to create room for arm movement. Best of all, the lengths of the front and back need not match.

The shaped Twister Ponchette requires just one hank of yarn and is shown in the colorway Potluck Brights.

Skill Level: Easy

Finished Size: 24" x 17" without fringe

Gauge: 4½ sts = 1" in St st

MATERIALS

~1 hank of Twister from Cherry Tree Hill (75% merino wool, 25% superwash; 586 yds; 8 oz) in color Potluck Brights (**3**)

~24" and 29" size 9 circular needles

~4 stitch markers (1 should be a different color than the others)

~Size G/6 (4 mm) crochet hook

~Stitch holder

~Tapestry needle

SHAPE NECK

Note: *Slip markers as they appear in the rows.*

Ponchette is worked from the neck down.

With shorter needle, loosely CO 84 sts. Join in the round, being careful not to twist sts. Later, when work becomes too large for short needle, transfer sts to longer needle.

Base rnd: K12 (shoulder), pm, K30 (back), pm, K12 (shoulder), pm, K30 (front), pm (use different-colored marker for beg of rnd).

Rnd 1: Knit, inc in st before and after each marker by knitting front and back of st. You will have total of 8 inc.

Rnd 2: Knit even.

Rep rows 1 and 2 until you have 42 sts in each shoulder section and 60 sts in front and back sections for total of 204 sts. Poncho should measure about 5" long.

Next rnds: Knit even for 4" for total length of 9".

DIVIDE FOR FRONT AND BACK

K19, BO 4 sts for arm opening, K19, K60 back sts, K19, BO 4 sts for arm opening, K19, K60 front sts and first 19 shoulder sts. Your work will be divided into 2 sections: front and back. Place all back sts on st holder—98 sts.

SHAPE FRONT

Row 1: Cont in St st, work on front section only. BO first 2 sts as foll: sl 1, P1, psso, P1 and pass 2nd st over it, purl across.

Row 2 (RS): BO 2 sts as foll: sl 1, K1, psso, K1 and pass 2nd st over it, knit across.

Rep rows 1 and 2 until 2 sts rem. BO.

SHAPE BACK

Transfer sts from holder to needles and shape back as for front.

FINISHING

With RS facing you and using crochet hook and yarn, loosely sc 84 sts around neck opening. See "Single Crochet" on page 107. Block lightly with steam iron until edges lie flat. Cut fringe. Model is shown with 14" pieces folded in half and attached 2 at a time EOR with crochet hook.

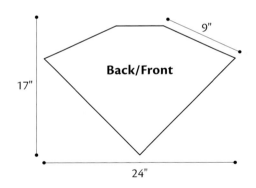

Circles SHAWL *By Kristin Omdahl*

This mohair bouclé knits loftier than sport-weight yarn usually does, and the yardage seems to go on forever. Kristin wanted to use it on a lacy openwork pattern to focus on the unique loopy texture of the bouclé. In openwork, going up a needle size usually makes a lacier fabric, but just the opposite applies to the elongated drop stitches she used. Once blocked, the crossed drop stitches opened up and the loops bloomed to create the illusion of concentric circles that Kristin desired. She recommends avoiding pointy needles because they tend to grab the mohair noils.

This wrap is knit in two halves from the side edge to the center and then joined with a three-needle bind off. The beauty of Baby Loop Mohair in garter stitch is that the seam is lost in the texture of the yarn. For best results, use a digital scale to divide the yarn in half before you begin.

This reversible wrap knits quickly with sport-weight yarn, and one skein is plenty. The Circles Shawl is shown in the colorway Spanish Moss.

Skill Level: Intermediate

Finished Size: 68" x 26"

Gauge: 5 sts = 1" in garter st unblocked or 4 sts = 1" in garter st blocked

MATERIALS

~1 hank of Baby Loop Mohair from Cherry Tree Hill (100% mohair; 965 yds; 8 oz) divided into 2 equal balls, approx 4 oz each in color Spanish Moss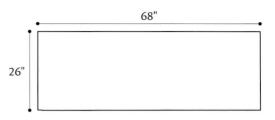

~29" size 7 circular needle

~Cable needle

~Tapestry needle

~2 stitch holders

~Digital scale for dividing yarn (optional)

RECTANGLE (Make 2)

CO 178 sts.

Row 1: Knit.

Row 2: K2, *K1 and sl back to LH needle. With RH needle, lift next 8 sts, 1 at a time, over this st and off needle, YO twice, knit original st again, K2, rep from * to end—82 sts.

Row 3: K1, *K2tog, drop first YO of previous row, (K1, P1, K1, P1) into second YO, K1, rep from * to last st, K1—98 sts.

Row 4: K11, (K1f&b, K14) 5 times, K1f&b, K11—104 sts.

Rows 5–16: Knit.

Row 17: *YO 3 times, K1, rep from * across.

Row 18: *(Sl 1 st to RH needle, drop 3 YO from previous row) 4 times, sl 4 sts from RH needle to cable needle and let fall to front of work, (K1, drop 3 YO from previous row) 4 times, K4 sts from cable needle, rep from * another 12 times—104 sts.

Rows 19–158: Work rows 5–18 another 10 times.

Rows 159–164: Knit.

Place all sts on holder.

FINISHING

Referring to "Three Needle Bind-Off" on page 108, sew 2 rectangles tog to form shawl.

Wash, block, and let dry.

Putting-on-the-Glitz SOCKS *By Judy Sumner*

Can adult-sized socks be knit from just one 4-ounce skein of DK-weight yarn? That was the question I had for sock guru Judy Sumner, and she thought it was likely. Generally she likes to have at least 3½ ounces or 300 yards of yarn available, so we chose a hank of Super Glitz, which is a superwash merino yarn laced with a strand of glitter. The 4-ounce hank yielded 325 yards, and Judy found she had enough yarn left over that she could have knit even larger socks.

The picot hem does use extra yarn, because it is knit and folded over to create a doubly thick edge. If you know at the outset that you have less than the required yardage, you can forego the picot edge or knit it in a contrasting yarn left over from another project. This could work if you also knit the toes or heels in the same contrasting yarn. You might want to try it just for fun, because running out of yarn with this hank is unlikely.

Both the design and the stitch pattern emphasize the glitz in these Super Glitz socks. Putting-on-the-Glitz Socks are shown in the colorway Spanish Moss.

Skill Level: Intermediate
Size: One size fits up to size 10 adult woman
Gauge: 5 sts = 1" in St st

MATERIALS

~1 hank of Super Glitz from Cherry Tree Hill (100% superwash merino wool with a strand of glitter; 325 yds; 4 oz) in color Spanish Moss ②

~Size 3 double-pointed needles, set of 5

~Stitch marker

~Size E/4 (3.5 mm) crochet hook

~Tapestry needle

LACE PATTERN

Rnd 1: *K2, P7, K3, rep from * around.

Rnd 2 and all even rnds: Knit.

Rnd 3: *YO, K2, P2, P3tog, P2, K2, YO, K1, rep from * around.

Rnd 5: *K1, YO, K2, P1, P3tog, P1, K2, YO, K2, rep from * around.

Rnd 7: *K2, YO, K2, P3tog, K2, YO, K3, rep from * around.

Rnd 8: Knit.

CUFF

Using 4 dpn, CO 48 sts (12 sts per needle). Join, being careful not to twist sts, and mark beg of rnd.

Rnds 1–6: Knit.

Rnd 7 (picot row): *YO, K2tog, rep from * around.

Rnds 8–13: Knit 6 rnds.

Work lace patt until cuff measures approx 5½" from picot row or desired length. End with patt row 8. Knit across needle 1 and turn work.

DIVIDE FOR HEEL

Row 1 (WS): Sl 1, then purl rem sts across needles 1 and 4. Place all sts on one needle for heel, turn.

Row 2: *Sl 1, K1, rep from * across needle, turn.

Rows 3–25: Rep rows 1 and 2, ending with row 1.

TURN HEEL

Row 1: Sl 1, K13, skp, K1, turn.

Row 2: Sl 1, P5, P2tog, P1, turn.

Row 3: Sl 1, K6, skp, K1, turn.

Row 4: Sl 1, P7, P2tog, P1, turn.

Cont in this manner, working 1 more st before dec on each row until 14 sts rem. Knit across and beg gusset.

GUSSET

Rnd 1: With crochet hook, pick up 12 sts along side of heel flap, M1 in loop between heel flap and instep needle, work patt across 2 instep needles, M1 in loop between instep needle and heel flap, with crochet hook pick up 12 sts along other side of heel flap. Divide heel sts between needles 1 and 4. Work 1 rnd, knitting M1 st with last st on each side of gusset and maintaining patt on instep needles 2 and 3.

Rnd 2: On needle 1, knit to last 3 sts, skp, K1.

On needles 2 and 3, work lace patt.

On needle 4, K1, K2tog, knit rem sts.

Rnd 3: Work 1 rnd with no dec, always maintaining patt on instep.

Rep rnds 2 and 3 until heel needles (1 and 4) have 12 sts on each needle.

FOOT

Work around as est until foot length is 1½" less than desired length from back of heel.

TOE

Rnd 1: On needle 1, work to last 3 sts, skp, K1.

On needle 2, K1, K2tog, knit rem sts.

On needle 3, knit to last 3 sts, skp, K1.

On needle 4, K1, K2tog, knit rem sts.

Rnd 2: Knit.

Rnds 3–8: Rep rnds 1 and 2.

Rep rnd 1 until 4 sts rem on each needle. Combine sts from needles 1 and 4 onto one needle and sts from needles 2 and 3 onto another needle. Referring to "Kitchener Stitch" on page 107, use tapestry needle and yarn to graft toe. Make 2nd sock, counting rows to make sure it is the same size.

FINISHING

Fold cuff at picot row and hem loosely.

Never-Ending SHAWL *By Cheryl Potter*

One of the most deceiving hanks of yarn I have ever worked with is Oceania. It is a bouncy wool bouclé with a strand of glitter that comes in a hank that is just short of 14 ounces but yields about 1,440 yards. Considered sport yarn, it lofts when washed and although lightweight, can become dense if you use a small needle.

Using size 8 needles, I chose a simple diagonal knit-and-purl pattern stitch with a yarn over just before the center marker; the pattern stitch is then reversed. Once the diagonal pattern is established after the first 12 rows, the knitting becomes mindless. As the shawl got too big to be a shawl, I continued. As it got large enough for a couch throw, I considered binding off some center stitches but didn't stop knitting until two of my employees wrapped themselves in it with room to spare and convinced me it was getting too big.

This never-ending shawl grew to the size of an afghan before I gave up and bound off without using an entire skein of Oceania. It is shown in the colorway Old Rose.

Skill Level: Intermediate

Finished Size: Shoulder line 73", depth 52" after blocking

Gauge: 3½ sts = 1" in patt st after blocking

MATERIALS

~1 hank of Oceania from Cherry Tree Hill (100% merino wool with a strand of glitter; 1440 yds, 400 g) in color Old Rose (**2**)

~29" size 8 circular needle. (As the shawl gets bigger, you may want to use 2 circular needles, 29" long, or a longer circular needle.)

~Large stitch holder

SHAWL

Note: *On all even rows, patt is repeated until marker is reached. After marker, patt is reversed and repeated to end of row. All odd rows are purled across; slip markers as they appear in the rows.*

CO 4 sts.

Row 1 and all odd-numbered rows (WS): Purl.

Row 2: K1, YO, K1, pm for center of shawl, K1, YO, K1.

Row 4: K2, YO, K1, K1, YO, K2.

Row 6: K3, YO, K1, K1, YO, K3.

Row 8: K3, P1, YO, K1, K1, YO, P1, K3.

Row 10: K3, P2, YO, K1, K1, YO, P2, K3.

Row 12: K3, P3, YO, K1, K1, YO, P3, K3. Diagonal patt is now est.

Row 14: K3, P3, K1, YO, K1, K1, YO, K1, P3, K3.

Row 16: K3, P3, K2, YO, K1, K1, YO, K2, P3, K3.

Row 18: K3, P3, K3, YO, K1, K1, YO, K3, P2, K3.

Row 20: K3, P3, K3, P1, YO, K1, K1, YO, P1, K3, P3, K3.

Row 22: K3, P3, K3, P2, YO, K1, K1, YO, P2, K3, P3, K3.

Row 24: K3, P3, K3, P3, YO, K1, K1, YO, P3, K3, P3, K3.

Cont in est patt until length from center top to center bottom is 50" or desired length. You may stop at any time before 50", but knitting rows beyond 50" may mean you cannot finish with one ball of yarn! You should have between 280–300 sts, depending on row gauge. End with WS (purl) row.

Shape Neck at Top Border

Row 1: Work est patt until 10 sts before marker, BO 20 sts, work patt to end of row. Depending on desired length of your garment, you should have 130 to 150 sts left on each side. Place right front sts on holder and cont on left front sts.

Row 2 and all WS rows: Purl to 3 sts before neck edge, P2tog, P1.

Row 3 (neck edge): Sl first st, ssk, cont in est patt (there are no further YOs made).

Rep rows 2 and 3 until 1 st remains, BO. Attach yarn to neck edge of right front and work as for left front, reversing all shaping. Block to finished size.

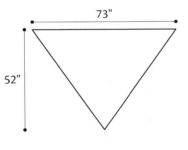

Vineyard SCARF *By Donna Druchunas*

Silk-and-merino yarns are some of my favorites, especially the single-strand versions, so supple and lustrous that they're a treat to knit. Scarves can be knit with almost any amount of yarn and are useful and stylish no matter what shape or size they become. Although easy to work with, this yarn is more slippery than wool. Using wood or bamboo needles will prevent you from losing stitches.

After reaching her goal of knitting a scarf 5' long, Donna had yarn left so she added fringe. Make this scarf any length you want, as long as you have 15 yards left to complete the end panel after knitting the drop-stitch section. If you like shorter scarves, you can knit two 30" scarves in this pattern from a single ball of yarn. If yardage runs short, simply rip out two or three drop-stitch panels until you have 15 yards to knit the end panel. You can also fringe this scarf with a solid-colored eyelash or ribbon yarn for an unusual accent.

Although silk and merino blends are expensive, this all-season scarf uses just one skein of yarn with plenty of yardage left for trim. The Vineyard Scarf is knit with Silk & Merino DK and shown in the colorway Martha's Vineyard.

Skill Level: Intermediate

Finished Size: Approx 6" x 60" without fringe

Gauge: 10 sts = 3" over netting stitch

Note: *Don't worry too much about getting the size exact. This yarn is extremely stretchy and will drape around your body beautifully, but it is impossible to measure accurately because it stretches in length or width depending on how you hold it.*

MATERIALS

~1 hank of Silk & Merino DK from Cherry Tree Hill (50% silk, 50% merino wool; 313 yds; 4 oz) in color Martha's Vineyard ⓷

~Size 10 needles

~Size G/6 (4 mm) crochet hook

NETTING STITCH

K1, *YO, ssk, rep from * to last st, K1.

SCARF

CO 20 sts.

Work netting st for 3".

Rows 1 (RS) and 2: Knit.

Rows 3–6: Knit.

Row 7: *K1, YO 3 times, rep from * to end.

Row 8: *K1, drop YOs, rep from * to end. Pull on bottom of knitting to elongate sts made from dropped YOs.

Rep rows 3–8 until scarf measures approx 57" long.

Work netting st for 3".

BO loosely, weave in ends.

FRINGE

Cut 44 strands of yarn, 12" long. Using crochet hook and 2 strands for each fringe, place 11 fringes along each short side of scarf. Netting-st panels should have open spaces that make it easy to insert fringe. Trim fringe for even edge.

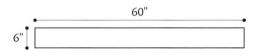

Ariel HALTER *By Celeste Pinheiro*

At 8 ounces and 475 yards, you wouldn't think one skein of this yarn would be enough to complete a garment. Celeste Pinheiro and I got together on a halter top design that could be longer for the smaller sizes and slightly shorter for larger sizes so that it was possible to knit the garment with one skein for all sizes without baring the midriff unnecessarily.

Celeste found that the 475 yards was ample for a size small as shown but that larger sizes would be shorter in length. She suggests that you knit the top as instructed and keep trying it on for length. If for some reason you end up with too many yards left over, you can always attach fringe to the lower edge with the extra yarn.

The bias knit hugs body curves, so if you want a looser fit, knit the next larger size to allow more room to adjust the back button. Because of the bias stretch and body-skimming fit of the top, gauge is less critical than you might think for this project.

This bias-knit halter top creates a body-hugging effect that can be adjusted by a button in the back. Ariel Halter is knit with Ariel and shown in the colorway Indian Summer.

Skill Level: Intermediate
Finished Bust: 31 (35, 39, 43)"
Finished Length: Approx 27 (26, 25, 24)"
Gauge: 20 sts = 4" in St st

Note: *For a close fit, take the actual bust measurement and subtract 5", and then choose the size closest to that measurement. For instance, if the bust measures 42", subtract 5" for a measurement of 37". You can then choose the 35" bust size for a body-hugging fit or the 39" bust size for more wearing ease.*

MATERIALS

~1 skein of Ariel from Cherry Tree Hill (65% cotton, 35% rayon; 475 yds; 8 oz) in color Indian Summer **2**

~Size 6 needles

~Stitch markers (6 short pieces of contrasting yarn for marking and measuring yarn for bottom band)

~1 large button, approx 1" diameter

~Sewing needle and thread for button

HALTER

Note: *This garment is knit from the top down. Before you begin, wind off 12 strands in 55" lengths to use for tie braids. Slip marker as it appears in the row.*

CO 45 (45, 53, 53) sts.

Row 1 (WS): Knit.

Row 2: *K2tog, YO; rep from * to last st, K1.

Row 3: Knit.

Row 4: K22 (22, 26, 26), YO, pm, K1, YO, K22 (22, 26, 26).

Next row (and all WS rows down to bottom band): K5, purl to last 5 sts, K5.

Cont in St st, keeping 5 sts on each side in garter st, making 1 YO on each side of marker on RS rows, inc as set another 31 (31, 39, 39) times—109 (109, 133, 133) sts, end with WS row.

Underarm Increases

Next row (RS): K5, M1, K49 (49, 61, 61), YO, K1, YO, K49 (49, 61, 61), M1, K5.

Cont in St st, make 4 inc EOR (2 center YOs plus 1 inc just inside each outside garter band) another 27 (37, 47, 57) times—221 (261, 325, 365) sts, end with WS row.

Next 10 rows: Work even along outside edges while cont to work center 2 YOs—231 (271, 335, 375) sts, end with WS row.

Before cont, you need to determine how much yarn is needed to complete bottom band. Tie 6 short pieces of contrasting yarn along yarn in 36" increments (start measuring yarn at your needle). Work next row, counting how many ties you pass as you knit. At end of row, round up to next tie. This tie count will be

number of yards you will need to complete bottom band. Multiply this amount by 10 to calculate yardage needed for band.

Keep knitting as in patt, and when ball dwindles to 8"circumference, cut yarn. Wind off yds needed, tie piece of contrasting yarn to mark yds needed, and then cont rewinding ball. Reattach yarn and cont, stopping after last WS row before yarn marker.

Next row (RS): *K5, K2tog, rep from * to last 7 sts, ssk, K5.

Cont in St st, dec 1 st on each side of every RS row and working 2 center YOs, (st count will rem same on each row) until you reach yarn marker you tied on yarn. End with RS row.

Bottom Band

Rows 1–10: Knit.

BO.

FINISHING

Take 6 lengths of yarn reserved for tie braids and fold in half. Push folded end through corner of CO edge to make loop and pull ends through as if you were attaching fringe. Now there are 12 strands. Separate into 3 sections of 4 strands each and braid to end. Tie knot at end and trim to make ends even.

Rep for other side. Try on halter top and pin in back to comfortable snugness. Using sewing needle and thread, sew button in place.

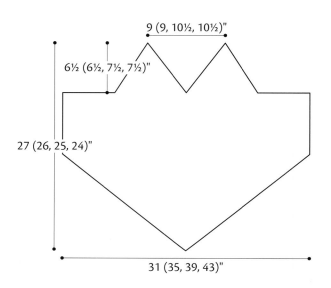

WORSTED-WEIGHT WONDERS

Worsted has long been the most common weight of yarn and what many beginners choose for first knitting projects. It is especially useful for teaching children to knit because it is thick and easy to handle, knits quickly on medium-sized needles, and is available in a huge array of colors and fibers.

As ubiquitous as it is popular, worsted yarn can be found anywhere from the most upscale yarn boutiques to discount department stores. Because of its universal appeal, worsted-weight yarn comes in a range of skeins from 1.75-ounce hanks to 16-ounce pull skeins. Most often it comes in bags of 6 or 10 in the same dye lot and the knitter chooses how many to buy for a project. Hardly anyone considers knitting an entire garment from just one hank; in fact, judicious knitters tend to overbuy for items such as sweaters and cardigans, afghans, and throws. Orphan skeins are common, and this section shows what knitters can expect from leftover balls. It may surprise you.

Various worsted-weight yarns

Child's Rolled-Top SOCKS *By JoAnne Turcotte*

With the challenge of knitting socks from one skein of worsted yarn, JoAnne's first decision was to limit herself to socks in just two sizes. Even then, she knew she would be cutting it close with the yardage. She found that the Super Worsted skein had enough to make socks but not a lot left over for the cuffs. To allow for maximum use of the yarn, JoAnne chose to make short cuffs that were not ribbed. She was able to produce these anklets in two sizes and found that the simple stockinette stitch accented the colorway in this smooth yarn.

If you choose to knit the smaller size, you can add an extra inch to the cuffs. JoAnne recommends bamboo double-pointed needles for this thicker yarn so that the stitches stay put.

Each pair of children's socks was knit from just one skein of Super Worsted merino wool. The smaller toddler socks are shown in the colorway Country Garden, and the larger child's socks are shown in the colorway Tropical Storm.

Skill Level: Intermediate
Size: Toddler (4 to 6, 8 to 10) years
Gauge: 5 sts = 1" in St st

MATERIALS

~1 hank of Super Worsted from Cherry Tree Hill (100% superwash merino wool; 215 yds; 4 oz) in color Country Garden or Tropical Storm (**4**)

~Size 5 double-pointed needles, set of 4

~Stitch marker

Note: When slipping stitches, always slip as if to purl except for ssk.

CUFF

With one needle, CO 32 (36, 40) sts. Divide onto 3 needles. Being careful not to twist sts, join and mark beg of rnd.

Rnds 1–7 (8, 9): Knit.

Rnds 8 (9, 10)–14 (16, 19): *K1, P1, rep from * around.

Rnds 15 (17, 20)–16 (19, 22): Knit.

DIVIDE FOR HEEL

Transfer sts around so that first 16 (18, 20) sts are on needle 1, and 8 (9, 10) sts on each of other 2 needles (needles 2 and 3). Work back and forth across needle 1.

Rnd 1: *Sl 1, K1, rep from * around.

Rnd 2: Purl.

Rnd 3: *K1, sl 1, rep from * around.

Rnd 4: Purl.

Rnds 5–16 (18, 20): Rep rnds 1–4.

Rnd 17 (19, 21): Rep row 1.

TURN HEEL

Row 1 (WS): Purl to 2 sts beyond center, P2tog, P1, turn.

Row 2 (RS): Sl 1, K5, K2tog, K1, turn.

Row 3: Sl 1, purl to 1 st before last turn, P2tog, P1, turn.

Row 4: Sl 1, knit to 1 st before last turn, K2tog, K1, turn.

Rep rows 3 and 4 until all sts at ends are used up, ending with RS row. There will be 10 (12, 12) sts left.

GUSSET

Cont to work with needle 1, PU 11 (13, 14) sts along side of heel. Knit across sts on needles 1 and 2. Using new needle, PU 11 (13, 14) sts along other side of heel, and cont knitting to center of heel sts—5 (6, 6) sts (needle 3). There should now be 16 (18, 20) total sts on needles 1 and 3, and 16 (18, 20) sts on needle 2. Center of heel is beg of rnd; needle 2 contains instep sts.

Rnd 1: Knit.

Rnd 2: On needle 1, knit to last 3 sts, K2tog, K1.

On needle 2, knit.

On needle 3, K1, ssk, knit to end.

Rep rnds 1 and 2 until there are 8 (9, 10) sts left on each of needles 1 and 3. Needle 2 will rem at 16 (18, 20) sts because no dec take place there. You will now be back to original number of sts. Beg to work in the round again, until length from back of heel is 1" less than desired length of finished sock or about 4 (5, 6)" long. At this point you can slip sock on to see length. Only toes should stick out.

SHAPE TOE

Rearrange sts on needles if necessary to get 8 (9, 10) sts on each of needles 1 and 3, and 16 (18, 20) sts on needle 2.

Rnd 1: On needle 1, knit to last 3 sts, K2tog, K1.

On needle 2, K1, ssk, knit to last 3 sts, K2tog, K1.

On needle 3, K1, ssk, knit to end (center of heel).

Rnd 2: Knit.

Rep rnds 1 and 2 until there are 20 sts left (5 sts each on needles 1 and 3, and 10 sts on needle 2).

FINISHING

Transfer sts from needle 1 to needle 3. Using 10 sts from needle 3 and 10 sts from needle 2, graft according to instructions in "Kitchener Stitch" on page 107. Anchor on inside; weave in ends.

Make 2nd sock, counting rows to make sure it is same size.

BEANIE and BOOTIES *By JoAnne Turcotte*

Several years ago, JoAnne Turcotte developed a penchant for knitting baby socks. When I first began dyeing cotton bouclé, of course she had to have it for socks, even though I thought this textured worsted weight yarn was too thick.

According to JoAnne, baby socks only take about 80 yards of yarn, and she was pleasantly surprised that her 4-ounce skein of cotton bouclé yielded 170 yards— plenty for a matching hat. Thus the beanie-bootie set was begun, and I cannot tell you how many sets I have personally knit for shower gifts. Because the yarn has so much bounce, we found that a simple stockinette stitch accented the colorway without detracting from the textured bouclé.

Both the baby hat and the pair of booties were knit from just one skein of Cotton Bouclé. The Beanie and Booties set is shown in the colorway Tropical Storm.

Skill Level: Intermediate
Size: 0–9 months
Gauge: 4½ sts = 1" in St st

MATERIALS FOR BEANIE AND BOOTIES

~1 hank of Cotton Bouclé from Cherry Tree Hill (100% bouclé cotton; 190 yds; 4 oz) in color Tropical Storm (4)

~Size 7 double-pointed needles, set of 4

~16" size 7 circular needle

~Stitch marker

INSTRUCTIONS FOR BEANIE

With circular needle, loosely CO 72 sts. Pm and join in the round, being careful not to twist sts.

Knit every rnd until total length is 5½", ending at marker. Change to dpns when needed.

Rnd 1: (K10, K2tog) around.

Rnd 2: (K9, K2tog) around.

Rnd 3: (K8, K2tog) around.

Rnd 4: (K7, K2tog) around.

Rnd 5: (K6, K2tog) around.

Rnd 6: (K5, K2tog) around.

Rnd 7: (K4, K2tog) around.

Rnd 8: (K3, K2tog) around.

Rnd 9: (K2, K2tog) around.

Rnd 10: (K1, K2tog) around.

Rnd 11: (K2tog) around—6 sts.

Rnd 12: K1, K2tog, K1, K2tog—4 sts.

Knit around on 4 sts for ½".

Cut yarn, leaving 6" tail; thread it through rem sts, draw up tightly, and secure. Weave in ends.

INSTRUCTIONS FOR BOOTIES
(Make 2)

Cuff

With 1 dpn, CO 24 sts. Divide evenly onto 3 needles (8 sts each). Join in the rnd, being careful not to twist sts, and mark beg of rnd.

Rnds 1–12: *K2, P2, rep from * around.

Rnds 13–14: Knit.

Divide for Heel

Transfer sts around so that there are 12 sts on needle 1, and 6 sts on each of needles 2 and 3. Work back and forth across needle 1.

Row 1: Sl 1, knit across.

Row 2: Sl 1, purl across.

Rows 3–12: Rep rows 1 and 2.

Row 13: Rep row 1.

Turn Heel

Row 1: Sl 1, P6, P2tog, P1, turn.

Row 2: Sl 1, K3, K2tog, K1, turn.

Row 3: Sl 1, P4, P2tog, P1, turn.

Row 4: Sl 1, K5, K2tog, K1—8 sts.

Gusset

Cont on needle 1, PU 7 sts along side of heel. Using new needle, knit across sts on next 2 needles (needle 2). Using new needle, PU 7 sts along other side of heel and cont knitting to center of heel sts (needle 3). There should now be 11 sts on each of needles 1 and 3, and 12 sts on needle 2. Center of heel is beg of rnd; needle 2 contains instep sts. Beg dec.

Rnd 1: Knit.

Rnd 2: On needle 1, knit to within 3 sts of end of first needle, K2tog, K1.

On needle 2, knit around.

On needle 3, K1, ssk, knit around.

Rep rnds 1 and 2 until there are 6 sts left on needles 1 and 3. Needle 2 will rem at 12 sts. Knit 10 rnds.

Shape Toe

Rnd 1: On needle 1, knit to last 3 sts, K2tog, K1.

On needle 2, K1, ssk, knit to last 3 sts, K2tog, K1.

On needle 3, K1, ssk, knit to end (center of heel).

Rnd 2: Knit.

Rep rnds 1 and 2 until there are 8 sts left. Cut yarn, leaving 12" tail. Draw yarn through rem sts. Draw up tight and anchor. Weave in all ends.

Sow's Ear MARKET BAG *By Donna Druchunas*

With lacy textures, smaller yarn amounts can be stretched to make larger bags. Donna used two different pattern stitches to create contrasts in texture and color repeats. The large drop-stitch panels in the bag stretch the yarn, and the netting pattern also provides a lot of mileage due to the open texture.

Although this worsted-weight yarn is easy to work with, the silk content can make it a little slippery. Use bamboo needles to avoid dropped stitches. The hairs from the mohair can catch into stitches as you knit, making it very difficult to rip out. The netting stitch has no plain rows, so take time to work slowly so that you can avoid mistakes and frustration. If you have to rip out a netting section, you will have to go all the way back down to the previous drop-stitch panel.

If yardage runs short on this bag, it's easy to use a contrasting yarn for the straps, which are knit last, or to substitute ribbon or leather cording for the straps.

A silk-and-mohair-blend yarn transforms this basic market bag into a luxurious accessory. Sow's Ear Market Bag is knit with Silken Mohair and shown in the colorway Winterberry.

Skill Level: Intermediate

Finished Size: Approx 13" wide x 15" high without straps

Gauge: Approx 12 sts = 4" in netting patt st

MATERIALS

~1 hank of Silken Mohair from Cherry Tree Hill (70% mohair, 20% silk, 10% wool; 424 yds; 8 oz) in color Winterberry (4)

~20" size 8 circular needle

~Size 8 double-pointed needles for handles, set of 2

~Stitch marker

~Stitch holder

~Tapestry needle

PATTERNS

Netting Pattern

Rnd 1: *YO, K2tog tbl, rep from * around.

Rnd 2: *K2tog, YO, rep from * around.

Rep rnds 1 and 2 for patt.

Drop-Stitch Garter Panel

Rnds 1 and 2: Knit.

Rnd 3: Purl.

Rnd 4: Knit.

Rnd 5: Purl.

Rnd 6: Knit.

Rnd 7: *K1, YO 3 times, rep from * around.

Rnd 8: *K1, drop YOs, rep from * around. Pull on bottom of knitting to elongate sts made from dropped YOs.

Rnd 9: Knit.

Rnd 10: Purl.

Rnd 11: Knit.

Rnd 12: Purl.

Rnds 13 and 14: Knit.

BODY OF BAG

Using circular needle, CO 80 sts. Pm, join, being careful not to twist sts.

Rnd 1: Knit.

Rnds 2–15: Work 14 rnds of netting patt.

Rnds 16–29: Work 1 rep of Drop-Stitch Garter Panel.

Rnds 30–57: Rep rnds 2–29.

Rnds 58–71: Rep rnds 2–15.

Divide front and back: K40. Place rem 40 sts on holder.

Front

Rows 1–3: Knit.

Row 4: K2tog, knit to last 2 sts, K2tog—38 sts.

Rows 5–7: Knit.

Row 8: Rep row 4—36 sts.

Rows 9–32: Work rows 5–8 another 6 times—24 sts.

BO.

Back

Transfer sts from holder onto needle. Attach yarn and work as for front.

Side Opening Edging

With RS facing you and using circular needle, PU 34 sts evenly spaced (17 sts on front and 17 sts on back) along opening on one side of bag. Knit 3 rows, BO.

Rep on other side.

HANDLES (Make 2)

1. Referring to "I-Cord" on page 108 and using dpns, work 3-st I-cord until I-cord measures 1".

2. Holding top front edge of bag with RS facing you and starting at left edge, work attached I-cord as foll:

   On row 1, K3, sl right needle into st on top edge of bag. You now have 4 sts.

   *Slide sts to other end of dpn.

   On next rows, K2, K2tog tbl, working 1 st from I-cord tog with st from top of bag. Sl needle into next st at top edge of bag. Rep from * until you can't pick up any more sts.

3. Work another 17" of unattached I-cord. BO. Cut yarn.

4. CO 3 sts. Work attached I-cord along top edge of entire strap, BO.

Rep for 2nd strap on top back edge.

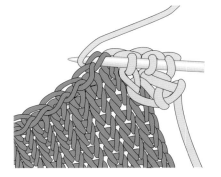

Note: *If you don't like to work attached I-cord, work the entire length of the strap in regular 3-stitch I-cord (see "I-Cord") and sew the pieces together.*

FINISHING

Using tapestry needle and yarn, sew ends of straps tog. Turn bag WS out and sew bottom seam. Weave in ends.

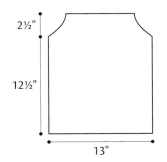

Shaped SHAWL *By Cheryl Potter*

When I knit a shawl from worsted-weight yarn, I like to have at least 500 yards to work with. Since the Silken Mohair had only 424 yards, I knew at the outset that I would have to make adjustments. This simple garter and lace pattern stitch is easy to knit and increases the surface of the shawl.

The other concession I made was a shaped neck and shoulder area. Here, after the shawl was as deep as I desired, I decreased the width of the shawl rapidly to create two triangular tails that could be tied in front or held in place by a fancy pin. Not knowing if there would be any yarn available for fringe, I left it to last. As it turned out, there was just enough yarn for sparse fringing. If yardage runs short, knitters can substitute a different yarn for fringe, but this shawl also looks great without fringe.

The secret to success with this shawl is the concave neck and shoulder shaping, which uses less yarn than a conventional shawl. Shaped Shawl is knit with Silken Mohair and shown in the colorway Moody Blues.

Skill Level: Beginner

Finished Size: Approx 15" neck and shoulder shaping, 58" from center back to tip without fringe

Gauge: 4 sts = 1" in patt st

MATERIALS

~1 hank of Silken Mohair from Cherry Tree Hill (70% mohair, 20% silk, 10% wool; 424 yds; 8 oz) in color Moody Blues (4)

~29" size 7 circular needle

~Size 7 (4.5 mm) crochet hook

~Stitch holder

PATTERN STITCH

Rows 1–7: YO, knit across.

Row 8: YO, *K2tog, YO; rep from * to last 2 sts, end K2.

SHAWL

CO 4 sts. Set up patt by working 1 row as follows (WS): YO, K4—5 sts.

Row 1 (RS): YO, knit to end—6 sts.

Rows 2–7: Rep row 1—12 sts.

Row 8: YO, *K2tog, YO; rep from * to last 2 sts, end K2—13 sts.

Rep rows 1–8 until you have 118 sts. You will be ending with row 1.

Note: *When row 8 is worked on each repeat, if there are not enough stitches left at the end to K2, end with K1 instead.*

Divide for Neck

Next row: YO, K52, BO 14 sts, K52. Place first half of sts on st holder and work second half of sts only.

Row 1: YO, knit to neck edge.

****Row 2:** BO 4 sts , knit to end.

Row 3: YO, knit to end.

Row 4: BO 4 sts, knit to end.

Row 5: YO, knit to 3 sts before neck edge, K2tog, K1.

Row 6: Sl 1, ssk, *K2tog, YO; rep from * to last 2 sts, end K2.

Row 7: Rep row 5.

Row 8: Sl 1, ssk, knit to end.

Rows 9–12: Rep rows 7–8 twice.

Rep rows 5–12 until 3 sts rem. BO.

Sl sts from holder onto needle. Attach yarn at neck edge. Beg at **, work same as other side.

FINISHING

Block shawl to finished size. With rem yarn, cut fringe into 10" lengths. Attach 2 strands of fringe at a time every 4th row by folding it in half and looping through row ends with crochet hook.

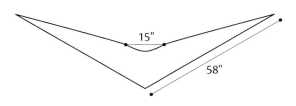

Alpine Lace WRAP *By Sharon Mooney*

One advantage of Alpine Lace is that it is a lacy bouclé with lots of bounce and it lofts well. Although this yarn is considered worsted-weight, it has so much body that it knits like a bulky yarn if you use large needles. Armed with size 15 needles, Sharon used an oblique openwork stitch and was able to create an ample wrap with just one skein of yarn. But she did use the entire hank and advises knitters to make certain they are knitting to gauge or be prepared to adjust the length of the shawl at the end of the project. If you run out of yarn before the garter edging, just rip out one repeat of the openwork stitch and use the yarn for the garter edge. When Sharon designed the wrap, she cut the fringe first. But if fringe is not important to you, use the extra yarn for finish work.

This openwork wrap is easy to knit and fun to wear. Alpine Lace Wrap is knit with Alpine Lace and shown in the colorway Blueberry Hill.

Skill Level: Intermediate
Finished Size: 50" x 23" without fringe
Gauge: 3 sts and 3½ rows = 1" in St st

MATERIALS

~1 hank of Alpine Lace (54% mohair, 23% silk, 18% wool, 5% nylon; 410 yds; 8 oz) in color Blueberry Hill (4)

~24" size 15 circular needle

~Tapestry needle

~Size H (5 mm) crochet hook

WRAP

If you desire fringe, cut 78 strands into 14" lengths and set aside.

Loosely CO 50 sts.

Rows 1–3: Knit.

Row 4 (RS): K6, *YO, K2tog, rep from * to last 6 sts, K6.

Row 5: K5, purl to last 5 sts, K5.

Row 6: K7, *YO, K2tog, rep from * to last 5 sts, K5.

Row 7: Rep row 5.

Rows 8–143: Rep rows 4–7.

Rows 144–146: Knit.

BO loosely. Cut yarn end to 6".

Weave in ends. Block wrap to finished size.

Fringe

Fold each length of fringe in half. Using crochet hook, attach 39 pieces evenly along each short side of wrap.

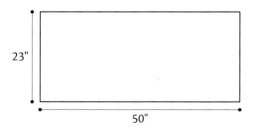

23"

50"

Knitter's Felted TOOL BAG *By Donna Druchunas*

For this project we chose Froth, a worsted-weight mohair bouclé with a touch of wool and nylon binder. Skeins are 8 ounces and more than 500 yards, so we knew there would be plenty for a medium-sized bag. Small bags can be made with 100 to 200 yards of mohair bouclé.

Froth requires a simple stitch pattern because the texture of the yarn obscures the stitches. Because the yarn is nearly impossible to unravel, simple stitch patterns also help knitters avoid mistakes. When the yarn is knit, the texture hides a multitude of mistakes, and felting the fabric will even close up small holes. The contrast between the furry texture of the felted bag and the frothy texture of the unfelted flap adds visual interest to the finished product.

If you run short on yarn for this project, try making the flap and strap out of a solid-colored yarn. Using wool instead of mohair would create a totally different texture and finished effect. Maybe try one of each just for fun!

This tool bag features a handy place for scissors and room for a tape measure in back. Knitter's Felted Tool Bag is knit with Froth and shown in the colorway Peacock.

Skill Level: Intermediate

Finished Size: Approx 10" x 10" before felting, 8" x 8" after felting

Gauge: 2 sts = 1" in St st using a double strand of yarn. Exact gauge is not critical. Make sure your knitting is loose and that you can see a little space between your sts.

MATERIALS

~1 hank of Froth from Cherry Tree Hill (88% mohair, 12% wool; 650 yds; 8 oz) in color Peacock (**4**)

~Size 10½ needles

~Size 10½ double-pointed needles, set of 2, for strap

~Tapestry needle

~Zippered pillowcase and mild soap for felting

~Size G/6 (4 mm) crochet hook for picking up stitches after felting (optional)

BODY OF BAG

Using single-pointed needles and double strand of yarn, CO 20 sts. Work in St st until piece measures 20". BO. Fold piece in half lengthwise. Using tapestry needle and yarn, sew side seams.

Optional Pocket

Using double strand of yarn, CO 10 sts. Work in St st until piece measures approx 5" and is square, BO. Center pocket on back of bag. Using tapestry needle and yarn, sew pocket to bag along bottom and sides.

STRAP

Referring to "I-Cord" on page 108, use dpns and double strand of yarn to work 3-st I-cord for approx 30", BO. Using tapestry needle and yarn, sew 2 ends of I-cord tog to form circle, then sew I-cord around top of bag, leaving excess 10" free for wrist strap.

FINISHING

Felt bag, referring to "Felting" on page 107.

Flap

With RS of bag back facing you and using double strand of yarn, PU 20 sts across back. If you have trouble getting sts through felt with knitting needle, use crochet hook to pick up sts, and then transfer them to knitting needle.

Work 8 rows in St st, end with WS row.

Row 1 (RS): K1, K2tog, knit to last 3 sts, K2tog, K1— 18 sts.

Row 2 (WS): Purl.

Rows 3–16: Work rows 1 and 2 another 7 times—4 sts.

Row 17: K1, K2tog, K1.

Row 18: Purl.

Row 19: K1, K2tog. BO.

Button and Loop

CO 1 st.

Row 1: K1, P1, K1, P1, K1 into single st.

Row 2: Purl.

Row 3: Knit.

Row 4: Purl.

Row 5: Sl 1, (K2tog) twice, pass first K2tog over second, psso—1 st rem. BO last st.

Use tapestry needle and yarn ends on button to sew it onto front of bag. Weave in ends. Cut 12" length of yarn and fold it in half. Adjust it to tip of flap to form button loop. Using tapestry needle and yarn, sew it onto tip of flap. Weave in ends.

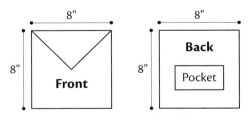

Measurements after felting

BEAUTIFUL BULKY WEIGHTS

It used to be that when I pictured bulky yarn, I imagined thick wool knit on large needles or craft yarn used for felting or rug making. In truth, bulky yarn can be composed of any fiber and often it is not the thickness so much as the texture or embellishment that gives the yarn bulk. Much of what we term novelty yarn actually fits into the bulky category. Synthetic yarns can be fringed with glitter, animal fibers can be brushed or knobby like Jumbo Loop Mohair, and the way they loft when knit can provide additional bulk. Then there are composite yarns, which are actually several thinner yarns twisted together into one yarn, such as cotton-rayon blends like Zebra Caribe.

The bulky category has become so overrun with newer and thicker yarns that the CYCA's standard yarn-weight chart even shows a super-bulky yarn category. Can you imagine knitting a thick-and-quick throw or shawl in a few hours with super-bulky chenille on size 35 needles? It's more than possible—many people do!

A wide variety of bulky-weight yarns

Sachet Rickrack SCARF *By Cheryl Potter*

With this simple scarf, an off-center rickrack stitch provides a fun exercise in color management. Sachet Rickrack Scarf is knit with Sachet and shown in the colorway Dusk.

Sachet is considered bulky even though it is composed of shiny nylon and looks weightless. It knits quickly and easily on large needles. The rickrack stitch pattern creates a sense of movement, because yarn is held in front or behind the needle depending on an odd or even row. The jaunty stitch echoes the bold lines of color in the fabric.

This scarf could be knit successfully from any number of wide ribbon yarns. With over 100 yards and size 13 needles, I knew there was plenty of ribbon for an ample scarf. Knitters who wish to use all the yarn may want to cut the fringe first and knit until about 2 yards from the end of the ball and bind off loosely. Another possibility for using more yarn would be widening the scarf, because it is already fairly long and does stretch. If yardage runs short, just remember to bind off after the second row of the repeat for a shorter scarf. The motif is based on a pattern stitch by Barbara Walker.

Skill Level: Easy
Finished Size: 50" x 8" without fringe
Gauge: 2 st = 1" in patt st

MATERIALS

~1 hank of Sachet from Cherry Tree Hill
(100% nylon; 142 yds; 4 oz) in color Dusk (5)

~Size 13 needles

~Size H/8 (5 mm) crochet hook

SCARF

With both needles held tog as one, loosely CO 16
sts, then pull one needle out, leaving all sts on rem
needle.

Row 1: P1, *YO, sl 1 wyif, P1, psso, rep from * to last
st, P1.

Row 2: K1, *YO, sl 1 wyib, K1, psso, rep from * to last
st, K1.

Rep these 2 rows for 48" or desired length of scarf.
Fabric will stretch. BO loosely. If desired, mist scarf
and block to measurements.

OPTIONAL FRINGE

For each end of scarf, cut 16 strands into 14" lengths.
Fold in half and use crochet hook to attach in sets of
2 to each end. Trim to even length.

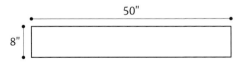

50"

8"

Evening SHAWL *By Cheryl Potter*

The standard-size skein for this yarn is 8 ounces, which yields about 500 yards. I found that 500 yards was more than enough yarn for this easy shawl. Although the high yardage may suggest that this fiber is a little thin for bulky yarn, the fact that it is highly brushed and lofts easily makes large-sized needles a must. Knitting too tightly will create a dense, matted appearance, and the garment may be uncomfortably warm.

This large triangular shawl has nice drape and plenty of air spaces to let the mohair loft and shine. The yarn-over increases create a pleasing eyelet edge. Be careful to avoid mistakes, because ripping out brushed mohair is almost impossible.

In order to maximize the yarn and use all of it, cut fringe first and then knit away until you have enough yarn left for the two eyelet rows and binding off. For an even larger shawl using the same amount of yarn, you can go up a needle size and fringe with contrasting yarn.

Just one skein of Brushed Mohair is used to create this large, simple eyelet shawl. Evening Shawl is knit with Brushed Mohair and shown in potluck purples and greens.

Skill Level: Beginner

Finished Size: 48" x 29" from center back to tip without fringe

Gauge: 2½ sts = 1" in St st

MATERIALS

~1 hank of Brushed Mohair from Cherry Tree Hill (100% mohair; 500 yds; 8 oz) in purples and greens (5)

~29" size 10½ circular needle

~Tapestry needle

~Size H/8 (5 mm) crochet hook

SHAWL

For fringe, cut approx 144 strands into 14" lengths before beg shawl.

CO 3 sts.

Row 1: YO, knit to end.

Rep row 1 until you have 150 sts.

Next row: K1, (YO, K2tog) to end.

Next row: Knit.

BO loosely and weave in ends.

FRINGE

Use crochet hook to attach 2 strands of fringe at a time by folding in half and looping through eyelet holes made by YOs. Trim to even length.

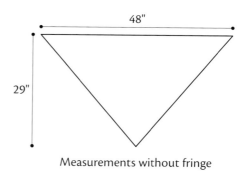

Measurements without fringe

Jumbo Flower SCARF *By Celeste Pinheiro*

Celeste chose to form the knitting of this scarf into a flower shape for a sculptural effect. She suggests using the flower motif as a pin, attached to a knitted hair band, or as embellishment on a sweater.

Using just one skein of Jumbo Loop Mohair, Celeste was surprised to find that she could knit 11 large flowers, too many for mere embellishment items. She tried knitting the flower in a bulky cotton yarn and was just as pleased. Celeste used all the 185 yards to knit the scarf shown, but estimated that 150 yards of bulky yarn would still produce an ample flower scarf. The Jumbo Flower Scarf would also make a fun scrap-yarn project, because alternating flowers of different textures and colors would emphasize the flower shape. We could even visualize it as a knitted lei—all you'd have to do is connect the ends and book a flight to Hawaii.

Although the original scarf was knit from heavy mohair bouclé, it works just as well in a light bulky yarn, such as cotton blend Zebra Caribe, shown here in the same colorway.

This innovative piece is knit in flower sections (shown below) and then linked together.

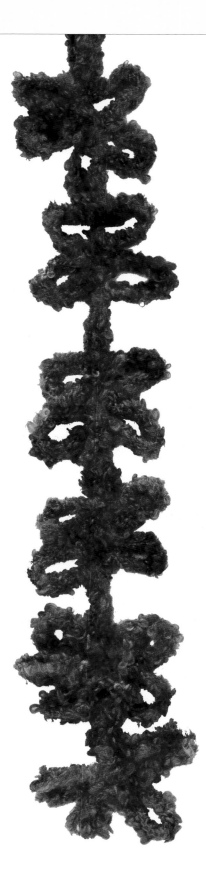

Skill Level: Beginner
Finished Size: Approx 66" long
Gauge: Not necessary

MATERIALS

~1 hank of Jumbo Loop Mohair from Cherry Tree
   Hill (88% mohair, 12% wool; 185 yds; 8 oz) in
   color Wild Cherry (5)

~24" size 10½ circular needle

~Sewing needle and thread

SCARF

CO 60 sts.

Row 1: Knit.

Row 2 (RS): *K1, BO 10 sts, K1, rep from * 4 times.

Row 3: Knit.

Row 4: K2tog across—5 sts rem.

Row 5: K5, cut yarn and pull tail through all 5 sts.

FINISHING

Using sewing needle and thread, tack flowers tog for
scarf as shown in diagram.

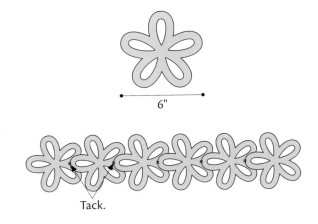

6"

Tack.

**Jumbo Flower Scarf is knit
with Jumbo Loop and shown
in the colorway Wild Cherry.**

Tuxedo SCARF *By Sharon Mooney*

Sharon designed this vest front so that it could be worn with a jacket to look like an entire vest but also cleverly function as a scarf. Sharon's Tuxedo Scarf only uses between 200 and 250 yards of yarn. Since Sharon had more yarn than that to work with, she did not need to halve the skein or avoid garter stitch, which works well with the textured bouclé and creates a fabric that is warm and practical as well as fashionable.

If you have more than the yardage required or you have too little yardage, you can easily make this scarf longer or shorter. Just remember to make sure the buttons are evenly spaced. If the yardage runs short, you can leave off one of the buttonholes, repeat one of the rows between the buttonholes, or both.

This innovative scarf buttons to form a faux Tuxedo vest front. Perfect for a night on the town, the Tuxedo Scarf is knit from Merino Bouclé and shown in the colorway Foxy Lady.

Skill Level: Intermediate

Size: Small (medium, large)

Neck Opening: 21 (25, 29)"

Gauge: Not necessary

MATERIALS

~1 Hank of Merino Bouclé from Cherry Tree Hill (99% merino, 1% nylon; 351 yds; 8 oz) in color Foxy Lady (5)

~Size 10 needles

~Tapestry needle

~5 buttons, ¾" diameter

~Sewing needle and thread for buttons

SCARF

Shape Buttonhole End

CO 2 sts.

Row 1: Knit.

Row 2: K1f&b, knit to end—3 sts.

Rows 3–13 : Rep row 2—14 sts.

Rows 14–19: (Rep rows 1 and 2) 3 times—17 sts.

Row 20 (buttonhole row): K1, K2tog, YO, knit to end.

Row 21: Rep row 2—18 st.

Rows 22–25: (Rep rows 1 and 2) twice—20 sts.

Rows 26–39: Knit.

Row 40: Rep row 20.

Rows 41–59: Knit.

Row 60: Rep row 20.

Rows 61–79: Knit.

Row 80: Rep row 20.

Rows 81–99: Knit.

Row 100: Rep row 20.

Knit every row for 33 (37, 41)" above buttonhole closest to needle. (Lay flat to measure; do not stretch.)

Let knitting hang down from needle. Buttonholes should be on left side as you look at scarf for next row. If buttonholes are on right side, knit 1 more row.

Shape Remaining End

Row 1: K1, K2tog, knit to end—19 sts.

Row 2: Knit.

Rows 3–12: Work rows 1 and 2 another 5 times—14 sts.

Rows 13–24: Rep row 1—2 sts.

BO.

FINISHING

Weave in ends. Block if necessary. Arrange scarf so that buttonholes are on right front as worn for woman's scarf or left front as worn for man's scarf. Match bottom edgings. Using needle and thread, sew buttons in place. Turn 2" of neck area to RS of scarf to make shawl collar if desired.

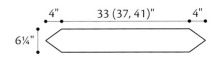

Glitter Knitter's BAG *By Donna Druchunas*

Donna thought this lacy pattern stitch would show off the texture as well as the glitter of the Glitter Thick & Thin. This yarn is easy to work with, because the wool offers plenty of give while the metallic thread holds the strands of yarn together, giving the stitches definition. Because the openwork stitch pattern saves yarn, we were able to make a larger bag than if we had used a tighter pattern stitch. The yarn has enough elasticity to work the decreases that form the diagonal lines easily and enough body that the bag holds its shape.

To be on the safe side, Donna divided the yarn into two equal balls so that she could see as she was knitting when to end the front and begin the back. That way she knew she would not run out on the second piece and that both sides would match. If yardage runs short, it is easy to knit the handles of the bag in a solid-colored yarn because the handles can be knit last.

This glitzy knitting bag offers enough room to stow a large knitting project. Glitter Knitter's Bag is knit with Glitter Thick & Thin and shown in the colorway Serengeti.

Skill Level: Intermediate
Finished Size: Approx 10" x 11" without handles
Gauge: 4 sts = 1" in garter st

MATERIALS

~1 hank of Glitter Thick & Thin from Cherry Tree
Hill (75% wool, 20% mohair, 5% metallic; 374 yds;
8 oz) in color Serengeti (5)

~Size 9 needles

~Tapestry needle

DIAGONAL LACE PATTERN

Row 1 (RS): *YO, ssk, rep from * across.

Rows 2 and 4: Purl.

Row 3: K1, *YO, ssk, rep from * to last st, K1.

Rep rows 1–4 for patt.

BAG

Front and Back (Make 2)

The bag is knit from the bottom up.

CO 40 sts.

Rows 1–12: Knit.

Work diagonal lace patt until piece measures 9½".

Shape Yoke

Rows 1–12: Knit.

Rows 13–14: BO 3 sts, knit to end.

Rows 15–24: K1, K2tog, knit to end—24 sts after
row 24.

Handle

Row 1 (RS): K4, BO 16 sts, K4.

Row 2: K4, CO 16 sts, K4.

Rows 3–14: Knit. BO.

FINISHING

Hem handle by folding handles in half so BO at
top of handle is lined up with top of hole. Using
tapestry needle and yarn, sew handle hem in place.
Sew side and bottom seams. Weave in ends.

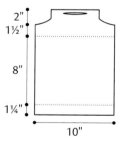

Alpamayo SHRUG *By Celeste Pinheiro*

Celeste designed this shrug as a basic knitted piece that could act as a template to be finished or embellished with other yarns. The first garment, Model A, is really nothing more than the basic body of the shrug knit from one skein of soft bulky-weight Alpamayo. Directions are to knit from the top down. As knitters run out of yardage, combining or adding yarns is easy. The basic body of the short-sleeve shrug takes about 160 yards.

Model A

In Model B, the shawl collar was added with an 8-ounce (173-yard) skein of Mohair Thick & Thin in the same colorway and knit until the mohair was gone. The sleeves were then lengthened with the Alpamayo until it, too, was gone. If knitters have more shawl-collar yardage and are able to keep going around, the collar could overlap more in front and become long enough in back to spread over the neck for winter weather. If you decide to do this, Celeste suggests increasing a needle size. If you change yarns while knitting sleeves, be sure to knit the same number of rows on each sleeve as you change yarns. Changing yarns on the shawl collar can create nice striping—just be sure to change at the beginning of a round.

The sizing on this garment depends on shoulder structure rather than chest size, resulting in a lot of flexibility in fit. For this reason, a shrug makes a great gift for someone when you are not sure about size, and the tie front makes the fit very forgiving.

Model B

Model A (above). The basic body of this short-sleeved shrug with knitted band is knit from one skein of Alpamayo, a bulky alpaca bouclé with barely 300 yards per skein in the colorway Spring Frost and embellished with optional Jumbo Flower (see Jumbo Flower Scarf on page 93).

Model B (left). One way to make this shrug larger is to embellish with a knitted shawl collar and long sleeves in coordinating yarn. Long-Sleeved Shrug with Shawl Collar is knit with Alpamayo and Mohair Thick & Thin in the colorway Spring Frost.

Skill Level: Intermediate

Sizes: Small/medium (medium/large)

Finished Chest: Approx 32 (38)"

Gauge: 12 sts = 4" in St st using size 10 needles

Note: This design has a lot of leeway in fit. To choose the correct size, measure snugly just under the underarm and above the bust.

MATERIALS FOR MODEL A
(Short-Sleeved Shrug)

~1 hank of Alpamayo from Cherry Tree Hill (48% alpaca, 48% wool, 4% nylon; 305 yds; 8 oz) in color Spring Frost (5)

~Needles: Sizes 9, 10, 10½, and 13

~Large stitch holder

~Stitch marker

~Tapestry needle

~Jumbo flower (Optional. For instructions see Jumbo Flower Scarf.)

INSTRUCTIONS FOR MODEL A
(Short-Sleeved Shrug)

With size 10 needles, CO 42 (46) sts.

Row 1 (WS): Purl.

Row 2: K2, YO, K9, YO, K1, YO, K18 (22), YO, K1, YO, K9, YO, K2—48 (52) sts.

Row 3: Rep row 1.

Row 4: K2, YO, K11, YO, K1, YO, K20 (24), YO, K1, YO, K11, YO, K2—54 (58) sts.

Row 5: Rep row 1.

Cont in est patt making 6 inc every RS row 13 (15) more times—132 (148) sts, end with WS row.

Left Sleeve

Row 1 (RS): K3tog, K39 (43). Transfer rem 90 (102) sts to st holder.

Row 2: Turn, purl.

Rows 3–8: Change to size 9 needles, work in K2, P2 rib for 6 rows, BO.

Right Sleeve

Leave next 48 (56) sts on holder for back. Transfer rem 42 (46) sts to size 10 needles. Work as for left sleeve.

Shape Back

Transfer 48 (56) sts from st holder to size 10 needles.

Row 1 (RS): Knit to last 3 sts, turn.

Row 2: Purl to last 3 sts, turn.

Row 3: Knit to last 7 sts, turn.

Row 4: Purl to last 7 sts, turn.

Row 5: Knit to last 12 sts, turn.

Row 6: Purl to last 12 sts, turn.

Row 7: Knit to last 18 sts, turn.

Row 8: Purl to last 18 sts, cut yarn.

Band

Row 1: With size 10 needles and RS facing you, join at left underarm. Knit across 48 (56) back sts, PU 45 sts along left front to beg of back neck, PU 18 (22) sts across back neck, PU 45 sts along right front edge, pm—156 (168) sts.

Rows 2 and 3: (K2, P2) across.

Rows 4–6: Change to size 10½ needles (K2, P2) across.

With size 13 needles, BO loosely.

Finishing

Using tapestry needle and yarn, sew sleeve seam. For ties, cut 6 strands of yarn about 55" long. Using 3 strands, double and attach as in photo, braid to length desired, rep on other side.

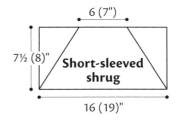

MATERIALS FOR MODEL B
(Long-Sleeved Shrug with Shawl Collar)

~1 skein of Alpamayo from Cherry Tree Hill (48% alpaca, 48% wool, 4% nylon; 305 yds; 8 oz) in color Spring Frost (5)

~1 skein of Mohair Thick & Thin from Cherry Tree Hill (69% wool, 28% mohair, 3% nylon; 173 yds; 8 oz) in color Spring Frost (5)

~Needles: Sizes 9, 10, 10½, 13, and 15

~Large stitch holder

~Tapestry needle

INSTRUCTIONS FOR MODEL B
(Long-Sleeved Shrug with Shawl Collar)

Note: Instructions include the option for three-quarter-length sleeves.

Using Alpamayo yarn and size 10 needles, work as for Model A until left sleeve. Divide rem yarn into 2 balls; use smaller ball first (if you can weigh them).

Three-Quarter-Length Sleeves

Left sleeve: On row 1 (RS), K3tog, K39 (43). Transfer rem 90 (102) sts to st holder.

On rows 2–13 (17), cont in St st, dec 1 st each side every 4 rows 3 (4) times.

On rows 14 (18)–31 (41), cont in St st, dec 1 st each side every 6 rows 3 (4) times—28 sts.

Change to size 9 needles and work in K2, P2 ribbing until 17" from CO edge at neck, BO.

Right sleeve: Leave next 48 (56) sts on holder for back. Transfer rem 42 (46) sts to size 10 needles. Work as for left sleeve.

Long Sleeves

Left sleeve: Work rows 1–31 (41) as for three-quarter-length sleeves.

Cont in St st until 17" from CO edge at neck, end with WS row.

On next row, change to size 9 needles and work in K2, P2 ribbing until 23" from CO edge at neck or until ball runs out, BO. (You may want to place sts on holder and BO after other sleeve is done to make sure both sleeves measure same length).

Right sleeve: Leave next 48 (56) sts on holder for back. Transfer rem 42 (46) sts to size 10 needles. Work as for left sleeve.

Finishing

Using yarn and tapestry needle, sew sleeve seam. For long sleeve, leave first 3" of cuff seam open; then sew sleeve seam.

Shawl Collar

Using size 10 needles and Mohair Thick & Thin yarn, PU as for band and work 2 rows in K2, P2 ribbing.

Inc row: Change to size 10½ needles, (K2, P2) once (twice), *K1, M1, K1, P2, rep from * 9 (10) times, (K2, P2) 10 times, K2, **P1, M1, P1, K2, rep from ** 5 times, (K2, P2) to end—172 (185) sts.

Next row: Work as set (knit the knit sts and purl the purl sts as they face you) for 5 more rows.

Next row: Change to size 13 needles, (knit the knit sts and purl the purl sts as they face you) for 6 more rows.

Change to size 15 needle, BO loosely.

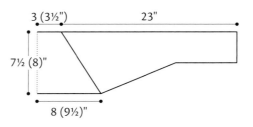

Salvaging Your PROJECT When SKEINS RUN SHORT

In "Common Yarn Weights and Yardages" on page 6 you are given estimates for how much yarn a project will require and how much yardage to expect from different kinds of yarn. From the project materials lists and instructions, you may have noticed which pattern stitches require lots of yardage and which pattern stitches stretch yardage. Armed with this information, you can recognize and avoid pitfalls that hamper the completion of a project with a given amount of yarn. Knitting with a limited amount of yarn takes planning. There may be sections of a garment that must be knit first or saved until last. Fringe might need to be cut, balls divided in half, or yarn weighed on a scale before knitting begins.

Why do some of our projects remain unfinished, sentenced to life in the knitting basket due to lack of yardage? Unfinished projects can be discouraging. Many knitters feel overwhelmed by the thought of ripping out a garment that has required so much time and effort. Often it seems impossible to salvage certain projects, when the truth is that almost any knitting can be saved. Remember that unfinished knitting is not like burnt toast. Although the toast might be ruined, the knitting can always be picked back to a certain spot and supplemented with other yarns. This section shows you how to rework various kinds of knitting projects and offers tips and advice from designers who contributed to this book.

SALVAGING SOCKS

Socks are some of the easiest knitted projects to salvage. If you haven't started knitting the socks yet but suspect there won't be enough yarn, the foolproof method is to divide your yarn in half and knit each sock from the toe up. This allows you to make shorter socks if necessary, and when the yarn does run out, it will be at the same place in each sock. You can then join a new contrasting yarn to create stripes or a pattern stitch, and it will look planned.

If you've already started the socks, knit them consecutively as in Potluck Supersocks on page 31. That way, you can use alternate yarns for any section of the sock—such as the heel, toes, or gusset—in the same place on both socks. If it is necessary to rip back one sock that is further along than the other, it may be worth it to have a completed pair of socks that look alike.

SALVAGING SCARVES

Scarves are also easier to salvage than you may believe. If you plan to add fringe with the same yarn, cut the fringe pieces first so that you can knit the scarf to the very end of the skein. If the scarf is already knit and you don't want to rip it back, consider forgoing fringe or fringing with an alternate yarn. If you are in the middle of a pattern repeat and run out of yarn, simply rip back to the end of the last pattern repeat and knit the finishing row or rows for a shorter but balanced scarf.

If you want to concentrate on length, make the scarf narrower than you had planned. You can make the scarf wider by finishing the entire scarf with a border in an alternate yarn.

Remember that you can cast on lengthwise rather than widthwise to ensure that you get the length you desire, and change yarns for a vertical stripe effect if you run out. If you are using a pattern stitch, use one with a short repeat to avoid being locked into an overly wide scarf that eats too much yarn. Drop-stitch patterns create a lacy look that uses less yarn.

SALVAGING SHAWLS

No matter what the shape, shawls can be saved. If you're knitting a triangular scarf and fear it will not be wide enough, consider knitting it from the top down. You can knit rectangular wraps or stoles lengthwise for the same reason. When opting for this method, make sure to cast on and bind off with larger needles than the pattern calls for. This will create sides with give that match each other. If you are certain you will run short, knit just the body of the shawl with your preferred yarn. If you cannot finish, knit borders with a contrasting yarn, or trim and fringe with an alternate yarn. Using horizontal bands of color or vertical stripes can add interest and stretch yarn at the same time.

SALVAGING OTHER GARMENTS

When knitting large garments such as sweaters or the Alpamayo Shrug on page 101, using top down construction is optimum for several reasons. If yardage runs short, it is easy to make the sweater shorter or to knit the ribbing or button bands with an alternate yarn. If you're knitting a conventional sweater from the bottom up and run out of yarn, take the cuffs and ribbing off and unravel them to finish the body of the sweater. You can always pick up and knit the cuffs and ribbing with a contrasting yarn.

If yardage is a concern, avoid involved pattern stitches and limit garter stitch—these all use a lot of yarn. Try to use openwork and larger needles if possible. Even plain stockinette stitch is easy on yardage. If possible, save the sleeves for last. If you knit them simultaneously, you can make them shorter. If you do not like the look of three-quarter-length or short sleeves, you can add stripes, side panels, or a long cuff in alternate yarn.

Special TECHNIQUES

FELTING

Put the item to be felted in a zippered pillowcase to catch the lint, and then put it in the washing machine with an old pair of jeans. Set the machine for the smallest load size with hot wash and cold rinse, and add 1 or 2 teaspoons of laundry detergent or no-rinse wool soap.

Check the felting every few minutes. When the fibers are matted and you don't want the item to shrink any more, take it out and gently rinse it in the sink. Roll the item in a towel and squeeze out the excess water. Dry flat.

KITCHENER STITCH

Cut the working yarn, leaving 18" for socks. Thread it onto a tapestry needle. Hold the two knitting needles parallel; you will now have a front needle and a back needle. Work with the tapestry needle and always keep the yarn beneath the needle as you work.

1. Go into the first sitich on the front of the needle as if to purl; leave the stitch on the needle.

2. Go through the first stitch on the back of the needle as if to knit; leave the stitch on the needle.

3. Go into the first stitch on the front needle as if to knit; pull the stitch off the needle.

4. Go into the second stitch on the front needle as if to purl; leave the stitch on the needle.

5. Go into the first stitch on the back needle as if to purl; pull the stitch off the needle.

6. Go into the second stitch on the back needle as if to knit; leave the stitch on the needle.

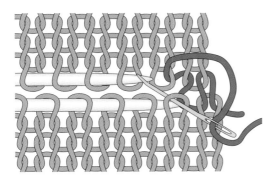

Repeat steps 3–6 until all sts are woven. Anchor on the inside and weave in ends.

SINGLE CROCHET (SC)

Single crochet is often used to join seams or finish edges. A crocheted seam lies flat and adds little bulk. To single crochet, insert the hook into the knit or crochet stitch. Place the yarn over the hook and draw it through the stitch. You now have two loops on the hook. Place the yarn over the hook and draw the yarn through both loops on the hook. A single crochet stitch is complete.

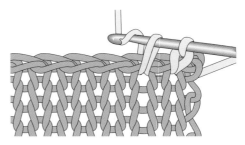

Insert hook into stitch, yarn over hook, pull loop through to front, yarn over hook.

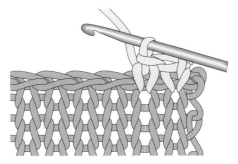

Pull loop through both loops on hook.

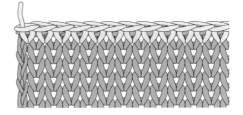

FRINGE

To attach the fringe, fold the two strands in half, insert the crochet hook from the back to the front as shown, hook the tail ends of the fringe, and pull them through the loop formed at the folded end of the fringe. Pull tight to secure.

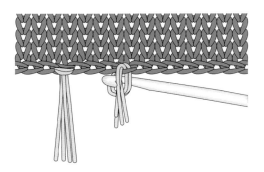

I-CORD

Knitted cord is often called I-cord, and it is made using double-pointed needles, although a circular needle can also be used. This cording is handy for making shoulder or purse straps for the Cascade Cover-Up on page 43 or the Knitter's Felted Tool Bag on page 83. Handles for the Sow's Ear Market Bag on page 73 were also constructed with I-cord.

Row 1: CO 2, 3, or 4 sts, according to project instructions.

Row 2: Knit all sts, but do not turn work. Slide sts to other end of needle.

Next rows: Rep row 2 until cord is desired length; BO. Cut yarn, leaving 6" tail; thread it through rem sts, draw up tightly.

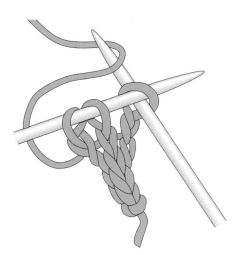

THREE-NEEDLE BIND OFF

The three-needle bind off is used to join seams in one step, rather than binding off both sets of stitches and then sewing them together, and it results in a less bulky seam.

1. Place the knitted pieces right sides together, with needles parallel and pointing in the same direction.

2. Knit two together (one st from the front needle and one stitch from the back needle). Repeat, and then pass the first stitch knit over the second stitch to bind off one stitch. Continue in the same manner until all stitches have been bound off.

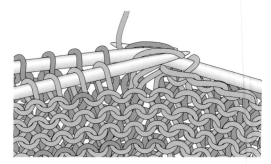

Knit together 1 stitch from front needle and 1 stitch from back.

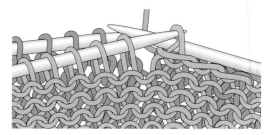

Bind off.

ABBREVIATIONS and GLOSSARY

approx	approximately
beg	begin(ning)
BO	bind off or bound off
ch	chain stitch (crochet)
CO	cast on
cont	continue (ing)
dec	decrease(ing)(s)
dpn(s)	double-pointed needle(s)
EOR	every other row
est	established
foll	follow(ing)(s)
g	gram(s)
inc	increase(ing)(s)
K	knit
K1f&b	knit into front and back of same stitch—1 stitch increased
K2tog	knit 2 stitches together—1 stitch decreased
K3tog	knit 3 stitches together—2 stitches decreased
kw	knitwise
LH	left hand
m	meter(s)
M1	make 1 stitch
mm	millimeter(s)
oz	ounce(s)
P	purl
p2sso	pass 2 slipped stitches over
p3sso	pass 3 slipped stitches over
P2tog	purl 2 stitches together—1 stitch decreased
P3tog	purl 3 stitches together—2 stitches decreased
patt	pattern(s)
PB	place bead
pm	place marker
psso	pass slipped stitch over
PU	pick up and knit
pw	purlwise
rem	remain(ing)
rep(s)	repeat(s)
RH	right hand
rnd(s)	round(s)
RS	right side
sc	single crochet
skp	slip 1 knitwise, knit 1, pass slipped stitch over—1 stitch decreased
sk2p	slip 1 knitwise, knit 2 together, pass slipped stitch over the knit 2 together— 2 stitches decreased
sl	slip (slip all stitches purlwise unless instructed otherwise)
ssk	slip 2 stitches knitwise, 1 at a time, to right needle, then insert left needle from left to right into front loops and knit 2 stitches together—1 stitch decreased
st(s)	stitch(es)
St st	stockinette stitch or stocking stitch
tbl	through back loop(s)
tog	together
WS	wrong side
wyib	with yarn in back
wyif	with yarn in front
yb	yarn back
yd(s)	yard(s)
yf	yarn forward
YO(s)	yarn over(s)

Metric CONVERSIONS and Knitting NEEDLE SIZES

METRIC CONVERSIONS

m = yds x 0.9144

yds = m x 1.0936

g = oz x 28.35

oz = g x 0.0352

KNITTING NEEDLE SIZES

Millimeter Range	U.S. Size Range
2.0 mm	0
2.25 mm	1
2.75 mm	2
3.25 mm	3
3.5 mm	4
3.75 mm	5
4 mm	6
4.5 mm	7
5 mm	8
5.5 mm	9
6 mm	10
6.5 mm	10½
7 mm	10¾
8 mm	11
9 mm	13
10 mm	15
12.75 mm	17
15 mm	19
19 mm	35
25 mm	50

RESOURCES

Needles and Notions

Bryspun Needles

Bryson Distributing

www.brysonknits.com

Addi Turbo Needles

Skacel Collection Inc.

www.skacelknitting.com

Yarns and Patterns

Cherry Tree Hill

100 Cherry Tree Hill Ln.

Barton, VT 05822

www.cherryyarn.com

About the DESIGNERS

JUDY SUMNER is a retired gerontologist, but knitters know her as a whimsical sock designer. Her patterns have appeared in numerous books and magazines. In this book, she expands her repertoire to include children's wear, inspired by her twin granddaughters and the Smoky Mountains that surround her Tennessee Valley home.

BARBARA VENISHNICK was a nationally known designer from Connecticut. Her sudden death in 2005 saddened hand knitters around the world.

Self taught, **KRISTIN OMDAHL** began to knit and crochet while expecting her son. Eventually booties and blankets were no longer needed, so she began designing other garments and never looked back. Every free minute is spent designing contemporary knit and crocheted women's wear. To find out more about Kristin, contact her through her Web site at www.styledbykristin.com.

SHARON MOONEY prefers knitting to any other activity. At the age of seven, she knit her first project, a rug for Barbie. She has designed both cross-stitch and knitting patterns, and now owns a pattern company called Knitting Knoodle. She owns the Yarn Deli yarn shop in Redlands, California. Visit her on the Web at www.knittingknoodle.com.

JOANNE TURCOTTE is Design Director for Plymouth Yarn Company. She has been knitting for over 40 years and designing patterns for more than half of that time. JoAnne was trained and educated as a chemist, and she worked in materials engineering before finding her niche in the knitting world. In her spare time, JoAnne teaches knitting classes at a yarn shop near her home in Pennsylvania.

DONNA DRUCHUNAS lives near the foothills of the Colorado Rocky Mountains, where she spends most of her time writing and knitting. Her designs and articles have been featured in most of the major knitting publications, and she is the author of several books. Visit her on the Web at www.sheeptoshawl.com.

CELESTE PINHEIRO lives in the boondocks of McMinnville, Oregon. When she is not playing with yarn, she can be found puttering in her garden, listening to the wind, chopping the winter wood, or trying valiantly to keep up with her menfolk in the woods on her dirt bike.

Knitting and Crochet Titles

America's Best-Loved Craft & Hobby Books®

America's Best-Loved Knitting Books®

CROCHET

Creative Crochet NEW!

Crochet for Babies
and Toddlers

Crochet for Tots

Crochet from the Heart

Crocheted Socks!

Crocheted Sweaters

Cute Crochet for Kids NEW!

The Essential Book of
Crochet Techniques

Eye-Catching Crochet

First Crochet

Fun and Funky Crochet

**Funky Chunky Crocheted
Accessories NEW!**

The Little Box
of Crocheted Bags

The Little Box of Crocheted
Hats and Scarves

The Little Box of Crocheted
Ponchos and Wraps

More Crocheted Aran Sweaters

KNITTING

200 Knitted Blocks

365 Knitting Stitches a Year:
Perpetual Calendar

Big Knitting

Blankets, Hats, and Booties

Dazzling Knits

Double Exposure

Everyday Style

Fair Isle Sweaters Simplified

First Knits

Fun and Funky Knitting

Funky Chunky
Knitted Accessories

Handknit Style

Handknit Style II NEW!

Knits from the Heart

Knits, Knots, Buttons, and Bows

Knitted Shawls,
Stoles, and Scarves

The Knitter's Book
of Finishing Techniques

Lavish Lace

The Little Box of Knits for Baby NEW!

The Little Box of Knitted
Ponchos and Wraps

The Little Box of
Knitted Throws

The Little Box of Scarves

The Little Box of Scarves II

The Little Box of Sweaters

Modern Classics NEW!

Perfectly Brilliant Knits

The Pleasures of Knitting

Pursenalities

Pursenality Plus

Ribbon Style

Romantic Style

Sarah Dallas Knitting

Saturday Sweaters

Sensational Knitted Socks

Silk Knits NEW!

Simply Beautiful Sweaters

The Ultimate Knitted Tee

The Yarn Stash Workbook

Our books are available at bookstores and your favorite craft, fabric,
and yarn retailers. If you don't see the title you're looking for, visit us
at **www.martingale-pub.com** or contact us at:

1-800-426-3126

International: 1-425-483-3313 • Fax: 1-425-486-7596 • Email: info@martingale-pub.com